Central and East European Economies in Transition

Central and East European Economies in Transition

The International Dimension

András Köves

Westview Press
BOULDER • SAN FRANCISCO • OXFORD

All rights reserved. No part of this publication may be reproduced or transmitted in any form or by any means, electronic or mechanical, including photocopy, recording, or any information storage and retrieval system, without permission in writing from the publisher.

Copyright © 1992 by Westview Press, Inc.

Published in 1992 in the United States of America by Westview Press, Inc., 5500 Central Avenue, Boulder, Colorado 80301-2877, and in the United Kingdom by Westview Press, 36 Lonsdale Road, Summertown, Oxford OX2 7EW

Library of Congress Cataloging-in-Publication Data
Köves, András.
  Central and East European economies in transition : the international dimension / András Köves.
    p.   cm.
  Includes bibliographical references (p.   ) and index.
  ISBN 0-8133-8380-3 (hardcover). —ISBN 0-8133-1643-X (pbk.)
  1. Europe, Eastern—Economic policy—1989– 2. Central Europe
—Economic policy. 3. Europe, Eastern—Economic conditions—1989–
4. Central Europe—Economic conditions. I. Title.
HC244.K693 1992
338.947—dc20   92-19628
                                                          CIP

Printed and bound in the United States of America

  ⊗ The paper used in this publication meets the requirements of the American National Standard for Permanence of Paper for Printed Library Materials Z39.48-1984.

10 9 8 7 6 5 4 3 2 1

Contents

List of Tables   ix
Acknowledgments   xi

   Introduction   1

   The Legacy, 2
   External Indebtedness and Economic Crisis, 5
   The Impacts of Declining Soviet Power, 6
   Political Change and Economic Reorientation, 9
   The Five and the West, 11
   Notes, 14

1 Shock Therapy Versus Gradual Change: Economic
   Problems and Policies (1989–1991)   17

   Shock Therapy in Poland: Some Lessons and Implications, 20
   Other Experiences with Shock Treatment, 25
   Detour: German Reunification as Shock Therapy, 27
   The Case for Gradualism, 30
   Notes, 34

2 Dilemmas of Privatization   37

   Arguments for Rapid Privatization: A Brief Overview
     and Assessment, 37
   Privatization from a Broader Perspective, 40
   Some Principal Difficulties of Privatization, 41
   Giveaway Privatization: How and Why? 43
   Is It Really Speed That Counts? 45
   Notes, 46

3 Systemic Transformation and Foreign Economic
   Liberalization: Trade and Investment Issues   49

   Trade Liberalization in Practice, 50
   Foreign Direct Investment and Economic Transition, 52
   Notes, 57

4 The End of the CMEA: Implications of the Change
   to Dollar-Accounted Trade   59

   The End of a Trading System, 62
   Changing the System or the Currency of Trade? 63
   Transition Policies, 1989–1991, 65
   The Safety Net and the Problem of Transferable-Ruble
      Surpluses, 65
   Negotiating Transition, 67
   Policy Options for the Five, 71
   Notes, 75

5 Economic Integration and Cooperation in Postcommunist
   Central and Eastern Europe   79

   Economic Cooperation Versus Integration, 80
   Toward a "Small" Integration? 84
   "Small" Integration from an International Perspective, 90
   Notes, 92

6 "Joining Europe": A Thorny Path   93

   Opening Up to the World or Joining a Regional Integration? 93
   The European Community and the Five: Some Asymmetries, 94
   Association Agreements: On the Way to Joining Europe? 95
   Is There a Solution to the Dilemma? 100
   Notes, 101

7 Hard-Currency Debt and Western Policy   103

   Deterioration of the Debt Situation, 104
   "Marshall Aid" Versus IMF Conditionality, 108
   Financial Relations and Policy Priorities, 111
   The Five's Place: Inside Europe or at Arm's Length? 114
   Notes, 115

8 Outlook for the Five: External Constraints
   and Policy Options   119

   Debt Management and Transformation in Hungary, 120
   The Five and the End of the Soviet Union, 124
   Systemic Transformation: Learning by Doing, 127
   Notes, 130

Bibliography	133
About the Book and Author	139
Index	141

Tables

1.1	Inflation rates in Central and Eastern Europe	23
1.2	Output in Central and Eastern Europe	23
1.3	Unemployment rates in Central and Eastern Europe	25
4.1	The collapse of Soviet foreign trade with the Five in 1991	61
4.2	Oil imports from the Soviet Union by the Five, 1988–1991	68
4.3	Soviet foreign trade, 1980–1990	73
5.1	Geographical distribution of exports by the Five in 1937	86
5.2	Geographical distribution of imports by the Five in 1937	86
5.3	Geographical distribution of exports by the Five in 1989	87
5.4	Geographical distribution of imports by the Five in 1989	88
5.5	Commodity composition of the trade of the smaller CMEA countries in 1989	89
7.1	Hard-currency debt indicators, 1989 and 1990	105
7.2	Current account balances of the Five in convertible currencies	106
7.3	External positions of East European countries vis-à-vis Western commercial banks	107

Acknowledgments

This book summarizes my views on the first two years of economic transition in Central and Eastern Europe. The majority of the manuscript was completed in the summer and early fall of 1991 and updated in January and February 1992. Special thanks are due to my employer, KOPINT-DATORG (the Institute for Economic and Market Research and Informatics), Budapest, which made it possible for me to concentrate on writing. I am also grateful to my colleagues at the institute, László Csaba, Gábor Oblath, and László Szamuely, who read the entire manuscript and made many useful suggestions. Éva Havasi, Gyula Munkácsy, and Veronika Pásztori helped me by providing important data and materials. I am indebted to Ede Lovas for assisting in computations. Jennifer Mergy was most helpful in reading and improving the English text. Katalin Tamon completed the difficult job of typing the different versions of the manuscript in an excellent and highly professional manner.

I was encouraged to write the book by Susan McEachern of Westview Press. I am grateful for her advice and support during its preparation.

András Köves
Budapest, Hungary
February 1992

Introduction

The initial experiences of systemic transformation of the countries of Central and Eastern Europe collectively known as the Five[1] have been mixed at best. In spite of significant country-to-country differences in their initial economic and political situations, pretransformation economic systems, and government policies, all of them are characterized by economic decline, increasing political conflict, and social strains. What is more, even at this point, there is for the most part no clear political, economic and, legal conception of the means for further transformation, and the credibility of the various government programs for economic stabilization is not beyond question.

The difficulties are not at all surprising. Some early euphoria notwithstanding, to most analysts it was clear from the outset that positive change in the economic situation and systemic transformation would require more time than political turnabout. It is generally accepted that transition from a largely state-owned, centrally planned economy to a market economy with a private sector of significant proportions (what can be seen as the substance of systemic transformation) is an unprecedented task. As Stanley Fischer and Alan Gelb have put it, although

> most of the individual requirements for socialist economy reform have been faced before, in China, and in Latin American and African countries where the combination of a weak private sector, political monopoly, heavy policy-induced distortions and macroeconomic imbalance is not uncommon . . . the challenge [in Central and Eastern Europe] *is* unique, in its system-wide scope, in its political and historical context and in the speed of desired reform (Fischer and Gelb 1991, p. 184).

It is widely believed in the West that "things will have to get worse before they get better," and Central and East Europeans cannot really advance any strong arguments against this.

What was unforeseen, however, was the speed and depth of the economic deterioration and the inability of the governments of the countries concerned, whether they had formulated some version of radical shock therapy or not, to control the decline or slow the accumulation of social and political tensions.[2] The rapidity of the decline in economic activity and living standards and of the increase in the degree of uncertainty of existence for large segments of the population in the period following the political transformation from late 1989 through early 1990 are unprecedented by European or North American standards. There is no peacetime example in post–World War II Western history of anything like a 10–14 percent decline of total output in a single year (as happened in Bulgaria, Romania, and Poland in 1990), a 20–24 percent drop in industrial production (as happened in Poland and Romania), or a 28 percent reduction in real wages in the predominant state sector (as happened in Poland).[3] Contrary to expectations, 1991 proved to be a year of even more serious shock. According to preliminary data, the drop in industrial output ranged from 12–15 percent in Poland and Hungary to as much as 20–24 percent in Romania, Bulgaria, and Czechoslovakia. Decreases in gross domestic product (GDP) ranged from about 8–10 percent in Hungary and Poland to well above 10 percent in Romania and Czechoslovakia and 20 percent or more in Bulgaria. Consumer prices increased by about 35 percent in Hungary, more than 50 percent in Czechoslovakia (though most of this increase took place in the first half of the year), and about 70 percent in Poland; triple-digit inflation is firmly established in Bulgaria and Romania.

Unemployment has become a most serious social problem throughout the region. Not only are rates of increase alarming but absolute levels are becoming very high even by Western standards. Whereas in the previous year unemployment rates (except in Poland) had been in the 1–2 percent range, by the end of 1991 unemployment in many countries of Central and Eastern Europe had reached or was approaching 10 percent—almost as high as in southern Europe. Most of these countries lack the infrastructure that would be necessary to manage unemployment.

In some countries living standards deteriorated more in 1991 than in the previous year. Czechoslovakia, with at least a 20 percent drop in real wages, is a case in point. Although neither the absolute dimensions nor the growth rates of the severe commodity shortages in some countries (Bulgaria and Romania) can be quantified, the causes of the disappointment and pessimism among the population of Central and Eastern Europe will be perfectly clear.[4] People are being told that their countries are about to join Europe, but they rightly feel that what is happening to them is something very un-European.

The Legacy

The new governments of the five countries correctly argue that they have inherited inefficient, internationally noncompetitive, and backward economies. Previous regionwide economic decline and destabilization and foreign debt must certainly bear the lion's share of responsibility for the difficulties of transition. Furthermore, changing deeply rooted economic and political structures, policies, institutions, and even behavior patterns is a complicated task. What is more, systemic transformation not only is, by definition, a further destabilizing factor in already largely destabilized economies but also involves restructuring in the deepest sense (change in the actors, institutions, and modes of functioning of the economy, etc.).

It would, however, be incorrect to view these difficulties in terms of sweeping generalizations about these countries' socialist systems. Those systems were dissimilar in many respects and changed over time. For example, the Hungarian economic reform of 1968 abolished mandatory planning and central allocation of resources, and by the late 1980s, even prior to political change, it had definitely progressed toward domestic and foreign economic liberalization and marketization of its economy (see Gács 1991, Köves and Maraer 1991). Economic transformation in this country should therefore for the most part be approached in terms of continuity rather than discontinuity (for a dissenting view, see Kornai 1990). In Poland, the other reforming country, progress was much more constrained and the tasks to be accomplished after the political change more difficult, but like the Hungarian, this system was fundamentally different from the variants of the classical Stalinist economic system that have persisted in practically all the other countries almost to this day.

A related point is that, partly because of these systemic differences among the countries concerned, their economic performances in terms of the welfare and living conditions of their populations (and their political freedoms) were also quite different. Whereas living standards in some of the countries were miserable, the rise in real incomes and improvements in living conditions in other countries was considerable by their own historical standards. In Hungary, for example, the 1960s and 1970s are justly regarded as having produced one of the greatest increases in living standards in the country's history. Hungarians recognize that these standards are still a far cry from West European ones, but they know that there is much to be lost if economic decline persists.[5] In Czechoslovakia, where there was rigid central planning until the very end, the consumer market, at low prices, was relatively well balanced. In view of this, the familiar argument that, because of the injustice and inefficiencies of the old system, no price is too high for transition to a market economy, not only is an unpopular one in Hungary and elsewhere but misses some very important points.

It is common knowledge that the whole decade of the 1980s in most of the five countries under discussion was one of decline. The deterioration of living standards was country-specific, but it affected every country in the region quite independently of the absolute level of welfare. This decade-long process of deterioration and the obvious inability of the respective governing parties and governments to cope with it is an important part of the explanation for the sudden and complete disintegration of all of the apparently strong and stable party-state regimes of Central and Eastern Europe. At the same time, it is an important message for the new governments in the region: Their legitimacy or acceptance by their populations depends to a large extent on their ability to offer authentic programs for the resolution of the current crisis and for longer-term economic development and improvement of living conditions. Any program for economic stabilization and systemic transformation, any talk about the relative merits of shock therapy and gradual liberalization, monetary austerity, the rapidity of privatization, debt management, and the like must be considered in this context. It is clear from this that we must beware of any one-sided approach to the problems of stabilization and systemic transformation based on ideologically or theoretically set priorities and disregarding the whole complex of economic, social, and political issues involved. This book will offer some insight into this fundamental problem.

What we have been witnessing in the economic decline of the 1980s is the *general* decay of a whole region: stagnating or declining production, obsolete investment stock, damaged infrastructure, deepening ecological catastrophe, falling living standards, declines in health and education levels, increasing and sometimes unmanageable external indebtedness (or, as in Romania, a domestic economy ruined by debt repayment), and domestic imbalances. As a consequence of their deteriorating economic performance, the Five's role in international trade has also declined dramatically. Their share in world exports dropped from 4.3 percent in 1970 to 2.2 percent in 1989, whereas their share in world imports declined from 4.1 percent to 1.9 percent. The trends in trade with the Organization for Economic Cooperation and Development (OECD) have been similar, though the decline of their share in total OECD trade has been somewhat more moderate—from 1.5 percent to 0.8 percent in exports and from 1.4 percent to 0.9 percent in imports.[6]

Although national patterns of industrial structure, development levels, factor endowment, and economic systems and policies have been different and all the countries have had their own specific reasons for and modes of deterioration, the generality of the crisis clearly suggests that it is systemic or the result of system-induced policies. Changes *within* the system—even when (as in Hungary) they have implied significant modifications in the mode of functioning of the economy—have not been comprehensive enough to rescue the countries concerned from crisis.[7] This fairly general appraisal—shared by many in both the East and the West—of the roots of the economic deterioration is, from another point of view, the single most important argument for regarding systemic transformation as a precondition for lasting economic stabilization and development in Central and Eastern Europe.

We largely share this interpretation, but the unavoidable question of the *timing* of the deterioration and collapse suggests that it is not the whole story. Changes in the international economic situation of Central and Eastern Europe have influenced the economic development of the Five throughout this period, and this particular set of issues is the main focus of this book. There are two foreign economic problems of particular importance for Central and Eastern Europe's economic performance in the 1980s: increasing debt to the West and economic relations with the Soviet Union. Both remain of primary importance in the period of systemic transformation.

External Indebtedness and Economic Crisis

It is easy to understand why the various implications of external indebtedness are in the forefront of current economic and political discussion in and about Central and Eastern Europe. Any policy initiative must take the debt and the burden of servicing it into account. Although the debt situations of the Five differ, many governments are finding that the enormous size of the annual interest and amortization payments precludes consideration of any easing of austerity measures.[8] At issue in the discussion are not only present options for managing the debt but also past policies, including the question of who is "responsible" for it.

Under present circumstances this discussion tends to become overheated and is not very helpful in explaining the economic realities that underlie the indebtedness. Clearly, past policy mistakes—both the financing of flawed development projects with Western credits and the implementation of inappropriate macroeconomic policies that made external financing unavoidable—are largely responsible for the huge increase of Central and East European debt in the 1970s and 1980s. It is not at all easy to distinguish between the two.

Be that as it may, when money was cheap in the aftermath of the first oil crisis, many countries around the world considered incurring debt a sound policy. However, when interest rates soared in 1979 as a consequence of the anti-inflationary policies of the U.S. Federal Reserve Bank, the imagined advantages of incurring debt proved the most serious obstacle to economic development. It is clear that, on the whole, the emerging huge (relative to their export performance and financing capacities) indebtedness of the Central and East European countries is part of a global process and therefore cannot be attributed to national economic policies alone.

It should be borne in mind that foreign credits are the normal concomitants of the functioning of any national economy, and in a stage of rapid industrialization and opening up to the international economy external financing (inflow of financial resources and foreign investment) usually plays an important role in promoting economic development and structural change. The difficult question for the recipient countries, however, is how to use foreign resources efficiently. Clearly, this problem has not been solved in Central and Eastern Europe in recent decades. In other words, the roots of the debt problem lie in economic systems and policies in the broadest sense of these terms. Imports from the West have increased, but traditionally autarkic (CMEA-oriented) development policies and institutions have not allowed for significant and lasting growth of exports to the West. Consequently, efforts at political and economic opening to the international economy have led to serious indebtedness. It is no surprise that the most open countries of Central and Eastern Europe, Poland and Hungary, have accumulated the largest debts and that the only "successful" experiment in repaying the foreign debt, in Romania, has resulted in economic chaos and increasing political oppression. It was, moreover, as an unintended consequence of debt to the West that the decades-long one-sided economic dependence of these countries on the Soviet Union was gradually replaced by a more complicated system of external dependencies, with dependence on the West more important than that on the Soviets.[9] In short, the impact of increasing indebtedness to the West is important for an understanding of the developments that have led to political change and systemic transformation.

The tough talk about "responsibility" for the indebtedness misses another point. Except in some countries and for a very limited period of time, the net inflow of financial resources from the West has in fact been modest. Ironically, the accumulation of debt in the 1980s has taken place amidst a severe net *outflow* of resources from the heavily indebted countries of the region. For example, Hungarian gross debt between 1982 and 1990 rose from $10 to $21 billion, notwithstanding a net outflow of $4 billion in terms of cumulative noninterest current-account surplus (OECD 1991b). Between 1985 and 1990 the gross debt of the Five increased from $59 to $90 billion and their net debt from $51 to $80 billion (OECD 1991b). During that period, however, they accumulated a noninterest current-account surplus of about $26 billion, including a cumulative hard-currency trade surplus of $14 billion (ECE 1991b). From this it is apparent that a substantial part of the current debt burden is due to the persistence of high interest rates for most of the past decade.[10] Thus we can conclude that Central and East European indebtedness is a consequence of weak and inconsistent efforts at opening up these economies to the international economy in a global environment that has become unfavorable to debtors. To put it another way, the economic crisis of the 1980s, deeply rooted in the systemic inefficiencies of Soviet-type economies, was precipitated partly by global developments.

The Impacts of Declining Soviet Power

The onset of the crisis, however, was mostly due to developments *within* the Soviet bloc. The single most important external influence on the economic and political fate of Central and Eastern Europe was the gradual decline, beginning in the mid-1970s, of Soviet economic power and performance, accelerating in the 1980s and combining with political disintegration to end in the total collapse of the Soviet Union itself. This economic decline was important in the Soviet Union's gradual disengagement in Central and Eastern Europe. Although its domination of the region depended primarily on military and political tools, economic relations always played an outstanding role arising from its economic and financial strength and its willingness and ability to supply its allies with oil, other energy, and raw materials. In exchange, Central and Eastern Europe contributed manufactures and agricultural products developed and produced especially for the Soviet market.

As an economically backward country (even relative to its European allies), the Soviet Union was of course never in a position to assist the small Central and East European countries significantly in their economic development. Contrary to the widely held view, intra-CMEA economic relations were *not* characterized by Soviet subsidization of the Central and East European economies.[11] Instead, the Five suffered substantial disadvantages from their involuntary participation in an autarkic bloc. The Soviet Union was, however, considered capable of influencing developments in its partner countries and even the fates of governing regimes through economic action (or inaction). This action used both stick and carrot, breaking off economic relations with such countries as Yugoslavia, China, and Albania following political schism and supplying both financial assistance and additional exports to Hungary after the 1956 uprising and in Czechoslovakia in the aftermath of 1968 intervention with a view to the political stabilization of the countries involved. In contrast, its avoidance of direct intervention in Poland in 1980–1981 and its inability to contribute in any perceptible way to the long-term stabilization of the Jaruzelski regime were of great significance for its subsequent relations with the whole of the European CMEA. Obviously, Soviet hard-currency loans and ruble clearing surpluses with Poland after 1981 served to prevent an instantaneous collapse of the regime but were clearly incapable of overcoming the difficulties caused by the enormous foreign debt and domestic decline. The process of reorientation in Central and Eastern Europe received new impetus, and the image of the Soviets as strong and reliable partners capable of helping the governments of Central and Eastern Europe to extricate themselves from economic or political difficulties gradually vanished.

The Soviet Union remained until recently, however, the single most important trading partner of each of the Five (according to the official statistics typically with 30 to 50 percent of their total foreign trade).[12] In 1990 and 1991, the Soviet economic collapse and the transition to dollar trade among the (former) CMEA countries led to an unprecedented decline in Soviet trade with the countries of Central and Eastern Europe that significantly contributed to the regionwide recession. Trade relations had, however, been gradually declining throughout the 1980s. In volume terms, Soviet deliveries of oil and other raw materials to Central and Eastern Europe had ceased to grow by 1979–1980 and decreased thereafter, and this undermined the very foundations of the traditional division of labor between the Soviets and their partners within the CMEA. With Soviet deliveries stagnating or falling, the economic rationale for a CMEA- or Soviet-oriented pattern of industrial development in those countries came to an end. Relations with the Soviets could no longer be regarded as a driving force and a guarantee of the traditional pattern of economic growth. In the first half of the 1980s this hard fact remained hidden as Central and East European terms of trade with the Soviet Union deteriorated in delayed response to the second international oil crisis (oil dominated Soviet exports, while manufactures were outstanding among the deliveries of the partners) and the logic of their bilateral clearing relations with the Soviets (the need for balanced trade) called for a dynamic increase in the volume of their exports to the Soviet Union.

This logic was, however, contrary to what the Five's economic situation required. Given their hard-currency debt, they needed more imports from the Soviet Union (to substitute for imports from the West) and/or less effort to increase traditional exports to the Soviet Union (to facilitate their reorientation to Western markets). Actually, at different times and in various contexts, all of the Central and East European governments declared their intention to rely more on Soviet trade as a way of avoiding indebtedness to the West. What followed was more exports to the Soviet Union (based, in large part, on investments of Western equipment in Soviet-oriented industries and the use of Western inputs in the production process), the largest Central and East European investments ever in Soviet energy (the Yamburg-Tengiz complex), and some hot air about new intra-CMEA cooperative projects corresponding to Soviet internal development plans. Needless to say, as the Soviets proved unable and/or unwilling to increase their deliveries, this policy resulted in *more*, not less, indebtedness to the West.

In the second half of the decade, terms-of-trade trends changed, again as a consequence of global oil-price developments. Under the conditions of improving terms-of-trade and declining Soviet deliveries, the Central and East European countries were confronted with a new and difficult choice. One possible alternative was to maintain the growth (or, at any rate, the level) of exports to the Soviet Union even though this meant increasing unusable clearing surpluses (i.e., outflow of resources) that would in turn increase imbalances in the domestic economy and/or trading and financial relations with the West. What was involved here was further hard-currency indebtedness for already heavily indebted countries. The other possibility was to cut back exports to the Soviet Union and insist on balancing bilateral trade and avoiding the outflow of resources. The problem with this choice was that most of the exporters of manufactured goods in these countries were highly (in many cases, exclusively) dependent on the Soviet market and unable to sell their products anywhere else. As exports to the Soviets represented a large proportion of national production, cutting back on those exports was clearly equivalent to economic recession, increasing unemployment, and social tension. It is no wonder that policy makers and enterprise managers were reluctant to choose this second alternative. They postponed the inevitable decision until it was too late (Köves 1990), and with the collapse of the Soviet Union a new shock to the already crisis-driven economies of Central and Eastern Europe could no longer be avoided.

What all this comes down to is that the continued dependence of the Central and East European countries on imports from and exports to the Soviet Union and the resulting subordination of economic strategies and tactics to the aims of developing bilateral economic relations with that country significantly contributed to the region's economic crisis. It should be clear that this contraction of trade was only the last straw. The wisdom of the one-sided (Soviet) orientation of their economic and trade development had much earlier, unintentionally and implicitly, been called into question by the Polish and Hungarian governments. They had realized as early as the 1970s that most of what they needed for the kind of technological and economic development that would ensure a lasting increase in living standards for their populations could be obtained only outside their relations with the Soviet Union (and outside the CMEA). Therefore they were ready to turn to the West for technology, financing, know-how, and (as far as Poland was concerned) even food. They were slow to realize, however, that any consistent outward-oriented policy was impossible without radical reorientation of their strategy of economic development and a shift from a planned to a market economy.

Political Change and Economic Reorientation

The difficulties of transition to outward orientation and integration into the international economy are well known. The liberalization attempts of many developing and newly industrializing countries all over the world (cf. Langhammer 1991) include some important successes, but so far the failures or doubtful outcomes are much more abundant. The important point is that, for the same reasons that systemic transformation is uniquely difficult in Central and Eastern Europe, strategic reorientation is much more complicated here than anywhere else. The CMEA- (Soviet-) oriented policies of the countries of this region were the product of the post-Yalta political and military division of the world. Any attempt (however halfhearted) at changing its foreign economic orientation on the part of any national government in Central and Eastern Europe was regarded by the Soviets as a violation of the international order and, consequently, opposed. At the end of the 1980s the Hungarians, as part of their economic reform plans, proposed a change from state trading to market-based relations with the Soviet Union (and other CMEA member countries). This change was intended to allow foreign economic reorientation of the country without challenging formal Hungarian participation in the CMEA, the (global) political status quo, or the continuation of cooperation of the traditional type among the other CMEA countries (Köves 1991). Before long the situation had changed, and the Soviets themselves launched a plan to shift from ruble to dollar trade among all the (then) CMEA countries. As a result, CMEA as a system of economic relations among its members was effectively abolished on 1 January 1991, the organization itself came to an end six months later, and its central power had ceased to exist by the end of the same year. There is no way to determine how realistic the Hungarian program of 1988–1989 was at the time. With the benefit of hindsight, it can be said that, in a sense, the Hungarian initiative was symptomatic of the approaching political change and systemic transformation, including the alteration of foreign trade regimes.

The political change in Central and Eastern Europe in 1989 and 1990 that removed the earlier political impediments to reorientation was a result of Soviet political decisions—even though its directions, speed, and consequences were from the outset beyond Soviet control. The decision to put an end to the Soviet bloc in Europe was one of the most important results of perestroika, in conformity with both its efforts at domestic democratization and the revision of Soviet foreign policy based on the postwar division of the world. Revision of the Soviet Union's global role became unavoidable because of its economic weakness. (It is not by chance that, in the subsequent period of decline of perestroika that culminated in the aborted coup d'état in August 1991, the decision to "give up" Central and Eastern Europe was among the most frequent targets of the conservative attacks.) A kind of a Soviet version of the theory of "implicit subsidies" according to which those countries were not assets but liabilities for the Soviet economy may also have played a certain role. Whatever the truth about Soviet–East European relations, this assessment, supported by official propaganda, made the decision easier. Given the destitute condition of the Soviet economy, the expected economic gains from disengagement seemed more important than the inevitable political and military losses. This was an important consideration in that the potential gains involved Western (German) assistance to the Soviet Union in exchange for its acceptance of German reunification.

Given economic collapse, the only verifiable economic result of withdrawal from Central and Eastern Europe for the former Soviet Union was a discontinuation of trade flows, which simply meant more shortages and deepening crisis in the domestic economy. It is no wonder that the idea of the economic integration of Central and Eastern Europe into the newly established system of intra-Soviet economic relations emerged in Moscow when Soviet and (mostly) Russian authorities addressed the issue of the economy in the aftermath of the defeat of the August 1991 coup.

It soon became clear, however, that the main problem facing the former Soviet policy makers was whether economic disintegration and the collapse of what had been the Soviet Union could be blocked or at least managed peacefully. The implications of the dismemberment of the Soviet Union for the economic relations between Central and Eastern Europe and the Soviet successor states and for the situations and policies of the Central and East European economies in transition will be dealt with at some length in Chapters 4 and 5. What should be underlined at this point is that even more than in the 1980s those relations continued to be constrained by economic and political collapse and disintegration in the former Soviet Union.

One can argue that the economic prospects for the various republics and regions of the former Soviet Union vary and some of them may have a relatively good chance of establishing economic relations with the Central and East European countries. Theoretically at least it may be appropriate for Central and East Europeans to focus on relations with these republics and regions. It is also true that there are some former Soviet regions that even today have their exportables (for example, Bashkiria, with its oil) and for that reason are especially important for Central and East European trade. The important point, however, is that economic prospects of *all* the successor states and territories (whether they belong to the Commonwealth of Independent States or not) are extremely uncertain, and this uncertainty is aggravated by the fact that unforeseeable political and other changes in the former Soviet Union seem as far from approaching an end as ever. One simply cannot know whether an agreement concluded today will remain valid tomorrow. In short, all the prerequisites—political, legal, economic, financial, personal, and so on)—for establishing stable trade relationships are lacking. What is more, Russia and (to a much lesser extent) the Ukraine account for the majority of Central and East European trade with the former Soviet Union, and therefore Central and East Europeans do not have free choice of trading partners among the successor states.

This severely limits the chances for a relatively short-term stabilization of trade between Central and Eastern Europe and the post-Soviet states (on whatever level). On the contrary, the trade collapse of 1991 in no way precludes further decline. This alone explains why talk of any kind of new integration of Central and East European economies with the successor states of the Soviet Union is counterproductive and, for the former, economic reorientation remains of the first importance.

The Five and the West

From the point of view of the issues to be analyzed in this book, the most important point is that the international political impediments to an opening up of the economies of Central and Eastern Europe to the international economy no longer exist. For these countries, one of the most important lessons of the past year or two is that freedom of international political movement and political reorientation does *not* lead automatically to economic reorientation and integration into the international economy. The external political prerequisites are only a few of the many preconditions for an opening up of the economy, and the others are various and difficult to fulfill. Domestic policies are the key to "joining Europe." What is needed is reconciliation of the tasks of economic stabilization and transformation with the maintenance and strengthening of the democratic order. The danger is that the combination of the real economic difficulties of transition briefly mentioned above with the more or less explicit intentions of some of the new governments in Central and Eastern Europe to return to pre-1945 systems and values and the resulting increase in social and political tensions will undermine both market oriented development and democracy. In view of ethnic conflict, the very survival of some of the present states in and around Central and Eastern Europe cannot be taken for granted.

In this situation, the responsibility of the West (the OECD countries, especially those of Europe) is enormous. Postcommunist Central and Eastern Europe depends on the developed Western countries for technology, investment, financial flows, export markets, management skills, and much more. It is only with Western support that the difficulties of adjustment related to the collapse of their economic relations with the Soviet Union can be eased. It is Western influence on the Central and East European governments, political parties, and other organizations that may help to curb their intolerant, antidemocratic, and aggressively nationalistic tendencies.

The difficulties for Western policy on Central and Eastern Europe are, however, immense as well. The first problem is, of course, the unavoidable differences in approaches and interests among the various Western governments, banks, international organizations, and so on, involved in Central and East European affairs. Developing any single Western policy with regard to the whole region or to individual Central and East European countries is an extremely difficult task. The second problem is the significance of the region for the West. At least until the onset of the crisis in Yugoslavia in June 1991, there were many signs of Western loss of interest in Central and Eastern Europe following the political changes of 1989 and 1990. According to some interpretations, what the West was really interested in was the fall of the Soviet bloc; subsequent events in the region seemed of marginal significance as far as global developments were concerned. There was a fairly general belief that nothing could happen here that would endanger Western stability—with the possible exception of an excessively rapid rapprochement and integration of the countries of the region with the West (the European Community [EC]). This suggested that the proper Western policy toward the countries of Central and Eastern Europe would be to keep them at arm's length. As absurd as it may sound, there have been clear signs of a preference on the part of important Western institutions and experts for reestablishing some version of the former bloc, including the former Soviet Union—at least in the economic field. This problem will be addressed in Chapter 5.

The dramatic events of the year 1991 should have effectively shaken some of the pillars of this way of thinking. The civil war in Yugoslavia has undermined the belief that the present condition of Central and Eastern Europe (and of its environment), its continuing economic decline, and its separation from "Europe" are consistent with the West's own requirements for stability. The abortive Soviet coup clearly demonstrated the inherent instability of the newly born world order. In fact, the defeat of the conservatives, amounting to what is generally perceived in both the East and the West as the end of communism (at least, in Europe), signified that the world had avoided a reemergence of the cold war—a development that could have been very dangerous for Central and Eastern

Europe. Nevertheless, the Western powers took the prevention of the political fragmentation of the Soviet Union as an important condition for international stability—an illusion that they gave up only with the Soviet collapse.

As has been mentioned, in the aftermath of the establishment of the Commonwealth of Independent States the future of the former Soviet Union is uncertain. To be sure, the international repercussions of this situation involve much more than the troublesome consequences for Central and East European trade. No one can tell whether political developments will continue to proceed as (relatively) peacefully as they have up to now or degenerate into serious armed conflict (among parties eventually possessing nuclear weapons). These internal uncertainties certainly contribute to a vagueness in the policies of Western governments and international organizations with regard to economic support of the new states. Although (somewhat belated) humanitarian aid to Russia and other former Soviet republics has been launched, the West remains uncertain about both the purpose and the possibility of offering meaningful financial support (at least for economic stabilization, debt management, and prevention of the collapse of oil exports) to the reforming post-Soviet economies. In early 1992 the basic Western dilemma seems as onerous and unresolvable as it was before the London summit in July 1991 or at any time thereafter. On the one hand, concerns about the chances of domestic reform and Western ability to enhance them through large-scale financial engagement in the former Soviet Union are valid and well founded. On the other, a policy of effective nonengagement (engagement limited to humanitarian aid) makes further disintegration and deterioration in the former Soviet Union a self-fulfilling prophecy. The London summit (rightly) rejected the idea of a "grand bargain" with the Soviet Union because its participants did not believe in Mikahil Gorbachev's ability to use Western help to prevent disintegration. Since then, however, the Union has effectively ceased to exist. In January 1992 Western governments may also be right in being skeptical about the chances of the Gaidar Plan in Russia and the economic and political future of all the republics and consequently putting off the difficult decisions about financial support. Most probably, the economic and political situation in the former Soviet Union will further deteriorate, and in the next round of deliberations concerning Western policy the costs and risks of *any* decision may be even greater than they are now.

We will strongly argue in this book that, for many reasons, including continuing uncertainty in Russia and other successor states and in Western relations with them, Western stakes in the political and economic stability of the Central and East European countries are much higher than is usually assumed. With this in mind, the most important point is that the means of fighting destabilization chosen by Western governments and international organizations in the past two years may prove counterproductive. It is from this perspective that the book will provide an assessment of the implications of EC attitudes toward Central and Eastern Europe (Chapter 6) and of Western financial and economic policy with regard to the region (Chapter 7). From the Central and Eastern European perspective, there is a need for change in Western policy in the direction of a more definite engagement in the region in the interests of both the East and the West. Western understanding of what is involved in systemic transformation in these five countries seems an important prerequisite for overcoming its difficulties. Needless to say, because economic transition in the former Soviet Union is only in its initial stage, better understanding of the policies and developments of transition in Central and Eastern Europe may also be helpful in advancing thinking about the means, constraints, and possibilities of the reforms there. This book is an attempt to contribute such an understanding.

Notes

1. For the purposes of this book, the countries of Central and Eastern Europe are Bulgaria, Czechoslovakia (renamed the Czech and Slovak Federal Republic), Hungary, Poland, and Romania. Systemic transformation in the former German Democratic Republic (GDR) is being carried out within the framework of a united Germany and is a somewhat different story. For the sake of comparison, however, we will refer to the German experience as well as to that of Yugoslavia. Yugoslavia and Albania are special cases for a different reason: Their history is different from that of the Five—Yugoslavia broke away from the Soviet bloc as early as 1948–1949 and Albania in 1961. We will refer to the Soviet Union and its successor states established as the Commonwealth of Independent States in December 1991 and to Soviet (and post-Soviet) economic problems as much as is necessary to understand the transformations and foreign economic dilemmas in Central and Eastern Europe. The Five, the GDR, the Soviet Union, and three non-European countries—Mongolia, Vietnam, and Cuba—made up the Council for Mutual Economic Assistance (the CMEA).

2. This statement refers also to the government of the Federal Republic of Germany.

3. It is widely argued that, as far as Poland is concerned, "the statistical real wage vastly overstates the actual decline in living standards" because "in 1989, goods were simply not available at the official prices. Queues and shortages were rampant. When prices went up in 1990, thereby eliminating the shortages and queues, the *real* effect on living standards was more modest than would seem from the official price statistics" (Sachs 1991, p. 242). But even if there has been substantial improvement in certain important aspects of living standards, the severe effects of cuts in real wages (on top of a long period of deteriorating living standards) should not be underestimated. Deteriorating living standards and the impoverishment of increasingly larger segments of the population and the resultant social strains and political disillusionment ultimately led first to the fall of the government of Prime Minister Tadeusz Mazowiecki and later to that of Deputy Prime Minister Leszek Balcerowicz, the "father" of the Polish reform.

4. For summary data on inflation, output, and unemployment, see Tables 1.1, 1.2, and 1.3 in Chapter 1.

5. In a poll conducted in Hungary in the 1970s, the most frequent reply to the question "what they were proud of most of all" was increase in personal well-being. Hungarian commentators were quick to add that the results of a similar poll in the United States showed that most Americans took the most pride in their political system.

Introduction 15

6. Computed from the *UN Statistical Yearbook* (for various years), the *UN Monthly Bulletin of Statistics* (1991/1), and the *OECD Monthly Bulletin of Foreign Trade* (various issues).

7. Although in some fundamental ways the crisis in Hungary has been markedly less than in most other countries.

8. Czechoslovakia and Romania are exceptions. The latter, however, though it has repaid practically all of its debt, is on the way to very serious indebtedness and difficulties in external financing at least as grave as those of the heavily indebted countries of the region. Czechoslovak indebtedness is also growing (see Chapter 7, Tables 7.1 and 7.2).

9. One of the first manifestations of this new situation was Hungary's joining the International Monetary Fund (IMF) and the World Bank in 1982. Hungary had intended to join the Fund as early as 1967, but it was only a decade and a half later that debt management problems made IMF membership a priority for policy makers and the Hungarian leadership ventured to ignore Soviet opposition.

10. Another not inconsiderable part of the debt results from the movements of exchange rates of the leading currencies.

11. The theory of "implicit" subsidies was developed by Michael Marrese and Jan Vanous (1983). See Köves (1983), for an early critical assessment, and Chapter 4.

12. These statistics clearly overestimate the Soviet Union's share, but its dominant role in the foreign trade of the Five is beyond argument.

1

Shock Therapy Versus Gradual Change: Economic Problems and Policies (1989–1991)

Despite significant ideological and political differences, the political elites of the new regimes in most of the Five came to power in 1989 and 1990 with the same firm belief: that they should establish a Western-type market economy with a significant or predominant role for the private sector to replace the Soviet-type planned economy with overwhelming state ownership.[1] Although proposals of some "third way" of economic and social development in Central Europe or at least some Central European countries (i.e., a pattern essentially different from both Western "capitalism" and Eastern "socialism") came to light time and again, their supporters proved unable to translate their ideas into practical terms and were therefore unable to challenge the general consensus over the transition to a market economy.[2]

The first question with regard to systemic transition is what kind of market economy the Central and East European countries have in mind. Theoretically, they might opt for the liberalism of the American experience, for some version of a more socially oriented West European market economy, or even for the sort of patriarchal market economy that exists in Japan and some newly industrializing countries. Various combinations of economic systems existing elsewhere are also feasible. Jeffrey Sachs maintains that arguments about the ends of transformation ("whether the aim for Swedish-style social democracy or Thatcherite liberalism") can wait: "Sweden and Britain alike have nearly complete ownership, private financial markets, and active labor markets. Eastern Europe today has none of these institutions; for it, the alternative models of Western Europe are almost identical" (Sachs 1991a, p. 235).

Clearly, problems of the means of the transition are much more urgent than those of the ends, but in many instances the two cannot be separated. For example, political decisions need to be made and legal measures adopted with regard to the development of a social safety net in the early stages of the economic transition. Conceptual problems of privatization also need to be settled as soon as possible, among them issues of privatization vs. reprivatization (returning property to its prenationalization and precollectivization owners) or restitution (total or partial compensation to former owners for lost property) and of differing approaches to support for the emerging private sector. The methods and the scope of privatization of state-owned firms will have a direct and long-term impact on the economic (and also the political and social) systems of the countries of Central and Eastern Europe as an outcome of the transition process. It is these long-term implications that are especially important and make present decisions about the strategy of the transition problematic. It would be naive to expect economic rationality to be the only guiding force of the transition, and this points to the most serious problem of all: Economic policies are being endangered by the implications of policy actions outside the scope of economic policy proper.

Quite apart from the political and other difficulties, however, the tasks of economic policy are immense, and "no single detailed road map can guide the way to the new systems" (Fischer and Gelb 1991, p. 189). In the words of the Polish economist Dariusz Rosati, "reading backwards existing Marxist-flavoured textbooks on the transition from capitalism to socialism" (1990, p. 2.) is not an adequate answer to the problems of transition. Unfortunately, sweeping generalizations of this kind are not uncommon both in the East and in the West. They imply, in one way or another, that the *speed of the transition* is what really counts and that speed is the single most important indicator of the success of government policies for transition.[3] The provocative agenda advanced by Rudi Dornbusch (1991) suggests that systemic transformation must be accomplished in seven days.[4] Although there are incontestably some strong arguments in favor of a rapid transition to a market economy, this way of thinking and the omnipotence attached to the pace of the transition neglects both the actual state of affairs in Central and Eastern Europe and the complexity of the issues that must be addressed. What is more, those who think along these lines "seem to forget that market reforms of these economies are not an end in themselves . . . economic growth is the goal of transformation process" (Brainard 1991, p. 95).

All of the economies in transition are facing many different tasks. Their most important and immediate task is *macroeconomic stabilization* (both external and internal). *Economic liberalization*—reducing the role of government in microeconomic decisions—must also be initiated or allowed to continue. This involves both liberalization of domestic policy and foreign economic relations (trade, investment, and finance). As is illustrated by the experiences of 1991, revamping intra-CMEA-type relations is a most difficult part of this latter aspect of liberalization. Finally, *privatization* is an essential feature of the establishment of a market economy, and this means both promoting the establishment and development of new private firms and privatizing state-owned companies.[5] As Lipton and Sachs (1990a) point out, "comprehensive action" is necessary on all those fronts. Obviously, these various economic-policy tasks are closely interrelated.

For example, the requirements of economic stabilization may in some respects contradict liberalization policies. More important, unless a long-term stabilization program is supported by systemic transformation from the centrally managed economy to one that is market-oriented, the danger of destabilization will persist. Structural reforms, in turn, can only work in a stable macroeconomic environment.[6]

Macroeconomic stabilization became the number one priority on the agendas of many countries as a consequence of the serious economic imbalances that had accumulated over the course of the past decade. Certainly this was the case with the two countries mainly concerned here—Poland and Hungary. External debt had accumulated rapidly since the mid-1970s in both countries. As early as 1980, Polish hard currency debt amounted to $24 billion, or 39 percent of the country's GDP, and its debt-service ratio was 96 percent (Szabó-Szuba 1991). In Hungary, gross debt in 1983 amounted to $11 billion or 57 percent of the GDP, and debt service was 47 percent of hard-currency exports (OECD 1991c). Protracted debt management difficulties made austerity measures unavoidable in both Poland and Hungary throughout the 1980s (austerity in Poland had begun even earlier). Hungary, however, has managed to service its debt, while Poland had to declare insolvency as early as 1981 and repeatedly rescheduled its debt throughout the 1980s. As a result, the decline in production and living standards was much more severe in Poland than in Hungary. Other differences related to the degree of internal disequilibrium also had a significant impact on economic decline and deteriorating living standards. Inflation accelerated in the 1980s in both countries. The inflation rate in Hungary remained a single-digit figure until as late as 1987, and the consumer price index did not exceed the 30 percent level in the difficult year of 1990. Polish inflation, however, turned into hyperinflation during the last months of 1989, the first months of the Solidarity-led government of Prime Minister Mazowiecki (see Kolodko 1991, Rosati 1990). Furthermore, because of earlier reform efforts and the growth of the private sector, domestic markets in Hungary have been more or less balanced (at least, by East European standards) and shortages of individual commodities more the exception than the rule. As a result, although discrepancies between the official and black market rates of the forint have often been as much as 50 percent, the domestic currency has retained the confidence of consumers and enterprises. In contrast, in Poland domestic markets were in total disarray in late 1989, and shortages of consumer goods were universal. In many fields the zloty was being squeezed out by the dollar, and in others consumers had to queue up for many hours a day to obtain basic necessities. This kind of shortage situation was and to a great extent remains characteristic of other countries, such as Bulgaria, Romania, and, of course, the former Soviet Union. It is important to note, however, that though the shortage phenomenon is explainable in terms of systemic factors,[7] the very high degree of excess demand and repressed inflation in Poland and some other countries during the period of political change in 1989–1990 must be attributed to the extraordinary depth of the economic decline and the weakness of preexisting economic policies. Furthermore, not only were the economic situations of the Five strikingly different but the same can be said of their domestic political situations. For example, in Poland "the new government came into power with broad public support, giving it an implicit mandate to introduce even a deeply unpopular program" (Köves and Marer 1991b, p. 21), whereas in Hungary public support for the Antall government was much weaker. In Bulgaria and Romania the political situation was even more complicated.

In sum, there can be no sweeping prescription or scenario for economic transition. Each country in transition to a market economy must have its own specific mix of actions aimed at macroeconomic stabilization, liberalization, and privatization. This is not to say that they cannot learn from each other's experiences. For example, the Polish experience in 1990 and 1991 is of great significance for all economies in transition.

Shock Therapy in Poland: Some Lessons and Implications

Poland was the first country in Central and Eastern Europe to announce a comprehensive and radical program of economic stabilization and liberalization. The program, linked to Deputy Prime Minister Leszek Balcerowicz, was initiated on 1 January 1990, and its philosophy and its content are as well known as the controversies surrounding its implementation.

The Balcerowicz Program was devised in cooperation with the IMF and other international experts and is regarded by the international community as the stabilization scheme par excellence for Central and Eastern Europe; subsequent programs for economic transition in other countries are being implicitly or explicitly judged, to a large extent, in its terms. The program represented genuine shock-therapy. Its authors were convinced that the conditions for long-term stabilization and systemic transformation could be established only at the cost of a serious *short-term* recession and decline in living standards. They were also certain that gradualism would not be successful. According to their way of thinking, as Rosati (1990, pp. 6–7) explains, "the tactics of extending the reform process over longer time leads invariantly to mounting resistance from conservatives and an erosion of support from the populace."[8] Further, they thought that a "piecemeal approach in implementing necessary changes" was "very likely to aggravate the overall economic situation and contribute to a decline of welfare level." Finally, "radical political changes" were needed "to allow for overcoming ideological constraints in the process of establishing new institutions and new power structure in the economy."

The Polish stabilization program aimed at eliminating excess demand in the economy once and for all and reducing the inflation rate to nearly 1 percent a month by the second half of 1990. Its most important distinctive feature as a stabilization scheme, however, was that rapid action on stabilization was intertwined with similarly radical liberalization. The instantaneous internal convertibility of the zloty as a result of its sharp devaluation was regarded as the cornerstone of the stabilization package.

The official zloty-per-dollar rate increased from 1,339 in September 1989 to 5,400 on 22 December and 9,500 on 1 January 1990.[9] At this rate internal convertibility was conceivable. Polish residents (firms and individuals alike) were allowed to exchange zlotys for convertible currencies with practically no restrictions. The zloty-per-dollar rate was fixed to serve as a nominal anchor in the ensuing process of economic stabilization and liberalization. In fact, the sharp devaluation allowed for the balancing of supply and demand for foreign exchange and a complete liberalization of imports (the removal of administrative restrictions in the allocation of foreign exchange). The package also included deep cuts in government expenditures (essentially subsidies) and a tight-money policy. Further, to prevent the reemergence of a wage-price spiral, a restrictive income policy was introduced, with prohibitive taxes on any increases in wage bills that exceeded predetermined indexation coefficients pegged to the inflation rate. Finally, dramatic price liberalization was introduced. By the end of January 1990, only 10 percent of prices were subject to any kind of administrative controls, as compared with 50 percent in 1989. The Balcerowicz Program was backed by external financial assistance including, among other things, a $1 billion stabilization fund provided by the OECD countries to support the internal convertibility of the zloty. No drawings from this fund have so far been necessary.

To assess the Polish stabilization program in an unbiased way, one has to distinguish between the ideology of the "big bang" and the Polish realities that produced the program. As has been indicated, radical shock therapy was advocated because of what Polish and international experts considered unfavorable experiences in Poland and other socialist countries with gradual reform. Reform failures must certainly be attributed, however, to various—mostly systemic—factors and political constraints and not simply to the inconsistencies of a gradual approach. Gradualism may mean very different policies depending on the circumstances. What is crucial is a clear distinction between stabilization and liberalization (or structural reform in general). Whereas a strong case can be made that in largely destabilized economies there is no alternative to bold surgery involving painful costs, there is no theoretical or empirical evidence to suggest that liberalization (especially external liberalization) must be equally rapid. Generally, attempts at economic liberalization in the international economy seem to provide more evidence for the advisability of the gradual approach. As Sachs (1989, p. 202) has put it,

> structural reform (especially a shift towards greater outward orientation and trade liberalization) is a very difficult process that takes many years to bring to fruition.

The process is so difficult economically and politically that it is likely to fail under the best of macroeconomic circumstances, and is in general greatly jeopardized by a concurrent macroeconomic crisis. The historical record suggests that stabilization should be given temporal priority in the design of adjustment programs, with structural reforms proceeding gradually and mostly *after* macroeconomic balance has been restored.

These points must have been overlooked in the preparations for the Polish stabilization *cum* liberalization program. It may well be that this was because of the weighty arguments in favor of one-time surgery *addressing specific Polish economic problems* in late 1989—serious domestic market disequilibria, a dual currency system, hyperinflation, and unmanageable foreign debt. Shock therapy was intended as a remedy for those ills. In this respect, and especially as a means of overcoming hyperinflation, its justifiability is beyond question.[10]

How efficient was this therapy? According to Rosati, "It seems unlikely . . . that the Polish experience may be successfully emulated in other countries where political environment is not so favorable. What is, however, much more important is that final results of the program are still to be seen, and the shock therapy has still to prove its long term viability" (1990, p. 11). Some Polish analysts assess the results of the stabilization program in downright negative terms (Kolodko 1991), whereas international assessments vary. Although some of the most important short-term objectives of the program have been fulfilled, other aims have been only partially and perhaps temporarily achieved. Most important, the price of these achievements has proved unexpectedly high. Consequently, Polish economic prospects continue to be uncertain.

The most important lasting change in the Polish economy is the elimination of excess demand. As a result of the stabilization operation of 1 January 1990, Poland was transformed practically overnight from a shortage economy into a demand-constrained one. For the first time in many years, even decades, Polish shops are full of commodities and queueing up as a way of life has disappeared.

Hyperinflation did come to an end, but inflation-rate targets have not been met. Not only did the anticipated "corrective" inflation of early 1990 related to price liberalization and the realignment of energy prices prove to be higher than planned but inflation was triple-digit and its monthly rate was about 4 percent in the second half of 1990 and higher in early 1991. According to preliminary data, in 1991 consumer prices apparently increased by 65–70 percent (see Table 1.1).

Internal convertibility has also worked. The zloty was devalued so sharply that, given its new level, no difficulties arose in balancing foreign-exchange demand and supply. It was not until May 1991 that, because of rapid inflation and worsening external balances, a new devaluation of the zloty was announced. The 1990 hard-currency trade surplus of approximately $4 billion and the resultant current account surplus is occasionally also considered an important achievement. It is, however, according to the Austrian economist Friedrich Levcik (1991, p. 4), "a questionable advantage for an impoverished country in the time

TABLE 1.1 Inflation Rates in Central and Eastern Europe
(percentage change in consumer price indices)

	1989	1990	1991[a]
Bulgaria	9.8	64.0	400–500
Czechoslovakia	1.4	10.1	58
Hungary	17.0	28.9	35
Poland	251.0	585.8	70
Romania	n.a.	n.a.	290[b]

n.a.: not available
[a] Preliminary estimates.
[b] October 1990–December 1991.
Source: OECD (1991d); KOPINT-DATORG estimates based on national data.

TABLE 1.2 Output in Central and Eastern Europe (percentage change)

	Net Material Product			Industrial Production		
	1989	1990	1991[a]	1989	1990	1991[a]
Bulgaria	−0.4	−13.6	−(20−26)	2.2	−14.1	−24
Czechoslovakia	1.0	−0.4[b]	−(12−14)[b]	0.8	−3.7	−23
Hungary	−0.2[b]	−4.0[b]	−(7−9)[b]	−2.5	−9.2	−15
Poland	−0.2	−11.6[b]	−(8−10)[b]	−0.5	−24.2	−12
Romania	−7.9	−10.5	−15	−2.1	−19.8	−22

[a] Preliminary. According to the official statistical sources, preliminary GDP data for 1991 in most countries are very uncertain. Therefore, they have, as a rule, announced GDP changes (declines) in a wide range.
[b] GDP.
Source: OECD (1991a, 1991d); ECE (1991b); KOPINT-DATORG estimates and projections based on national data.

of transformation." The surplus was certainly due to the country's deep recession (see Table 1.2).

Prior to examining this recession, one more important achievement of the program of stabilization should be identified. In the wake of long negotiations, Poland's creditors (especially the Western governments to which Poland owes most) have proved willing to forgive a large part of its debt. Given that the Polish debt has been by and large nonperforming for a decade or so, the agreement is not to be considered a favor to Poland. In fact it was mutually advantageous. For Poland the agreement made debt management feasible (though not easy) for the first time since 1982, and this is an important precondition for long-term stabilization.[11]

The consensus of Polish economists is that "the stabilization program actually overshot, producing excessive financial results obtained at excessive real costs" (Rosati 1990, p. 23). As has been indicated, to achieve convertibility the zloty was very radically devalued. Convertibility had to be sustainable, and consequently, given the isolation and disequilibrium of the economy, devaluation had to be much more extreme than "required by standard considerations related to stabilization policies" (Oblath 1991c, p. 7). Therefore, the austerity introduced as a means of restraining the inflationary tendencies inherent in devaluation also had to be more rigorous.[12] The result was an unexpectedly severe decline of domestic demand that could not be balanced by an increase in exports. Output fell sharply. For 1990 a 5 percent drop in industrial output, a 3 percent decline in GDP, and 1 per cent decline in consumption had been planned. In fact, GDP declined by 12 percent, returning to the level of 1984. What is more, because 1984 was a year of consolidation after the crisis of the early 1980s, the 1990 GDP was no higher than that of 1973–1974. In a single year domestic uses of the GDP declined by 17 percent (consumption by 24 percent and investments by 9 percent). As has been mentioned, living standards sharply deteriorated, and the industrial output of the socialized sector decreased by 23 percent. This decline certainly shows the weakness of the adjustment process in the state sector, a weakness that is very pronounced when compared with the dynamic growth of the private sector. The increase in the latter was 17 percent (in sectors other than agriculture 26 percent) in 1990. Its share in industrial production reached 13 percent. Despite the dynamism of the private economy, by the end of 1990 there were more than 1.1 million unemployed in Poland, comprising 6 percent of the labor force (KOPINT-DATORG 1991). Understandably, the initial strong domestic support for the Solidarity-led government gave way to strikes, political disillusionment, and social unrest. The strong support for the outsider candidate Stanisław Tyminski in the presidential elections of late 1990 was indicative of the profound change in the political atmosphere.

Contrary to expectations, unfavorable trends continued in 1991. For instance, output and real wages further declined. Preliminary data show a 8–10 percent drop in GDP and a 14 percent drop in industrial production compared with the previous year. Investment volumes sharply declined for the third consecutive year (10 percent as compared with 1990), real wages dropped by another 2–3 percent, and the trade surplus vanished. Inflation soared and unemployment increased, eventually exceeding 2.1 million. The rate of unemployment was the highest in Central and Eastern Europe (Table 1.3). If, as is often claimed, the previous year's decline in economic activity and incomes had been at least partly counterbalanced by the favorable effects of the end of the shortage economy and the internal convertibility of the zloty, in 1991 there was nothing to compensate the population for growing hardship and an almost intolerable deterioration of living conditions for a large number of people.

Largely as a consequence of social discontent related to the economic decline, the Mazowiecki government resigned, and the parliamentary elections in late 1991 were followed by the dismissal of Leszek Balcerowicz and his team of economic reformers. The new Polish government of Prime Minister Jan Olszewski came to power amidst the most serious attacks on austerity and promises of reflation. Should it stubbornly insist on fulfilling the policy changes

Shock Therapy Versus Gradual Change

TABLE 1.3 Unemployment Rates in Central and Eastern Europe (percent of labor force)

	December 1989	December 1990	April 1991	June 1991	December[a] 1991
Bulgaria	0.0	1.4	2.7[b]	6.0	10.0–11.0
Czechoslovakia	0.0	1.0	2.8	3.8	6.8
Hungary	0.5	1.6	2.9	3.9	8.3
Poland	0.3	6.1	7.3	8.7	11.1
Romania	n.a.	n.a.	0.6[c]	2.0–3.0	4.0–6.0

n.a.: not available
[a] Preliminary.
[b] March.
[c] According to ECE (1991b), the rate was 1.8 as early as January 1991.

Source: OECD (1991a, 1991d); KOPINT-DATORG based on official reports and national press.

promised during the election campaign, it could see the economy return to hyperinflation for which shock therapy would be the only solution. Most observers consider this latter unlikely, even if the government should prove unable (or unwilling) to resist the pressures for an easing of austerity. Indeed, the easing was initiated much earlier, by Balcerowicz himself. The important point is that two years after the shock therapy was launched and monetary austerity introduced, severe recession and high inflation persist, unemployment is on the rise, and the future of the economy is clearly uncertain. Thus continuation of the policies of the past two years is also not a promising alternative.

Other Experiences with Shock Treatment

As for the other Central and East European countries, it was their economic and political situation, which were different from Poland's, that led them to choose other approaches to transition. Nevertheless, pressures coming from different directions and the high priority attached to the speed of the transformation process, as well as the tremendous difficulties experienced with the gradual approach, have propelled many policy makers toward what is generally being called shock therapy. This is particularly applicable in the case of Bulgaria and Romania because of the near-collapse of their economies coupled with grave political uncertainties and a dramatic turnabout. Bulgaria has already embarked on its own version of shock therapy. Budget subsidies have been reduced, prices liberalized, and monetary austerity introduced. Imports in the first half of 1991 were one-third their level of the year before. The government argues that there is no alternative and that the Bulgarian population is capable of enduring a 50 percent cut in living standards (which, according to official sources, occurred in the first quarter of 1991) and other hardships.

Specifically, a radical move to introduce convertibility of their national currencies is frequently suggested for all the Central and East European countries.

Therefore, it is important to note that previous attempts at a rapid transition to convertibility in former socialist countries has not had lasting positive effects. Either the price to be paid for its introduction has proved very high (as in Poland) or it has failed outright (as in Yugoslavia) or what was called convertibility was merely the abolition of the all-pervasive system of administrative import licensing (as in Czechoslovakia). (However, for most of 1991, Czech and Slovak firms wishing to import commodities valued at more than Kč 6 million had to consult the national bank, and restrictions on purchasing foreign currency for purposes of tourism still apply.) In the most recent case, the Romanian, the introduction of internal convertibility in November 1991 did not even entail the effective abolishment of import licensing (it is the Romanian National Bank that disposes of the applications for imports).

Yugoslavia also faced hyperinflation in 1989, with the consumer price index increased by 1,256 percent.[13] This situation justified the Yugoslav version of shock therapy, the Markovic Program (named after the prime minister of the federal government). In all other facets the Yugoslav situation was dissimilar from that of Poland, especially in that there were no shortages in the domestic market. Inflation too was fed from different sources. Although the dinar was made internally convertible and tied to the deutsche mark, approximately 15–20 percent of imports remained under administrative control. A partial price and wage freeze was imposed for six months (in place of the wage indexing scheme that had existed in 1989).

By late 1990, the Markovic Program had collapsed. After the wage freeze ended in June, inflation accelerated and the current-account deficit soared. In response to the deteriorating economic situation (output was down by 8 percent in 1990), political developments were already threatening the country's very survival. The public lost confidence in the dinar and began converting dinars into deutsche marks on a large scale. To prevent the worst, free exchange of dinars into convertible currencies was stopped in the autumn. Subsequently, in December 1990, the government limited access to deposits in foreign-exchange accounts. As far as imports were concerned, the dinar officially remained convertible, but access to foreign-exchange accounts depended on the liquidity of the bank in which the accounts were held. The conditions of civil war and payments arrears led to the withdrawal of trust by the IMF and the international financial community. Even before the declaration of Slovenian and Croatian independence in June 1991 and the armed conflicts obscuring the future of what had previously been Yugoslavia, the likelihood of a reintroduction of convertibility was extremely slight.

However specific the reasons for the failed attempt at convertibility in Yugoslavia and the serious difficulties experienced in the Polish case, some relevant conclusions for the Five can be drawn.[14] Introducing convertibility is regarded by many experts and institutions, especially in the West, as the most important step in the external liberalization of Central and East European economies—in short, a sign of the seriousness of the reform programs of the governments concerned. To some extent, all of the Five's governments, whether opting for shock therapy or for gradual liberalization, are influenced by this approach. Convertibility must of course be introduced during the transition process, but attaching a high priority to introducing it at the outset is a mistake.[15] First, this approach ignores both the gradual establishment of convertibility in postwar Western Europe and the experiences of developing countries. Secondly, it concentrates on the technical side of the opening up of Central and East European economies instead of the more important economic processes that make such an opening possible—for example, reorientation of foreign economic relations, structural adjustment, and the development of international competitiveness—and thus ignores the real problems of external liberalization. Lastly, it neglects the recent experiences with the introduction of convertibility in former socialist countries. These experiences suggest that it is relatively easy to announce the establishment of some version of convertibility or to introduce internal convertibility in fact, and if the exchange-rate devaluation is deep enough the chances for *sustained* convertibility for some period of time will be strong. However, the price in terms of production and income loss is very high and makes the whole exercise questionable.

It should be clear that the deep recession and the resultant severe deterioration in living standards are not simply unfortunate by-products of the therapy applied. Much more is at stake. In sociopolitical terms, these developments may lead to an Argentine type trap instead of a West European or North American pattern of development. In terms of short- or medium-term economic policy, they would make adjustment impossible even in a normally functioning market economy. In a weak transitional economy, continuous sharp decline in domestic demand may create intractable adjustment difficulties not only for the state-owned sector, with its traditional rigidity, but also for the newly developing private sector. This is because there will not be enough capital at acceptable terms to finance business start-ups or enough customers capable of paying reasonable prices to make any undertaking rewarding. Governments too will face insoluble problems. Increasing unemployment will have to be financed largely from the budget, notwithstanding its having been sharply reduced. More important, austerity will inevitably lead to a retreat from liberalization and other structural reforms. Given the strong inflationary pressures and the impending (renewed) hyperinflation that are concomitants of the present economic situation in some of the Five, policy makers will have no alternative but to attempt shock therapy once more.

Detour: German Reunification as Shock Therapy

Besides Poland and Yugoslavia, there is a third well-known example of shock therapy in a former socialist country, the former German Democratic Republic. It is, of course, a special case of shock therapy in that systemic transformation there was taking place as a consequence of German reunification. What had been the GDR joined West Germany and became the five new *"Länder"* of the Federal Republic of Germany (FRG), adopting overnight its economic and legal system and its currency. The economy of the GDR as a national economy in its own right ceased to exist. This removed from consideration the problem of macroeconomic stabilization that is one of the most difficult aspects of systemic change. The considerable external indebtedness of the former GDR was assumed by the FRG, as was responsibility for monetary, fiscal, and social policy. West Germany, as one of the largest and richest economies in the world, was able to shoulder the burden of a much smaller and weaker economy (although the long-term macroeconomic impact of reunification is open to question).

Nevertheless, the short-term economic consequences of this particular mode of systemic transformation for the former GDR proved more shocking than in Poland or elsewhere. According to preliminary estimates, industrial production in 1991 was 50 percent below the level of the previous year and may not have exceeded 36 percent of the 1989 level, and unemployment (including part-time work) may have surpassed 3.5 million, more than 40 percent of the total labor force. Part of the explanation is consistent with the crisis in Central and Eastern Europe (for example, the collapse of the Soviet market [see Chapter 4]), but the depth of the shock was due to the specifics of economic reunification. Most important, not only did the transition to a market economy and an opening to the West German and international economies take place overnight, quite in the spirit of the "big-bang" theories, but also a special *revaluation shock* hit the East German economy. Convertibility was achieved in East Germany by introducing the deutsche mark in place of the mark. A one-to-one ratio was used for converting wages, other incomes, and smaller savings and a two-to-one ratio for converting larger money holdings and savings balances as well as enterprise assets and debt. For all practical purposes, the operation was tantamount to a significant revaluation of the East German currency.[16] It is not surprising that weak and internationally uncompetitive East German industries could not survive the shock.

Given the issues addressed in this study, two important questions should be asked. The first is whether the terrible short-term shock to the East German economy and population was unavoidable. Obviously, the manner in which economic reunification was achieved can only be explained in terms of the political considerations that made German unification pressing. Political reunification was to proceed quite quickly, and the commonly held view in the FRG was that economic reunification should take place parallel to it. (As a matter of fact, economic, monetary, and social union in July 1990 *preceded* political reunification.) Given the sad state of the East German economy the shock could have been avoided (or lessened) by integrating into the West German economy gradually. However, political circumstances did not allow for serious discussion of such an alternative. Conversely, the conversion rate of the mark into the deutsche mark was open to discussion before the union was established, for example, between the Bundesbank and the federal government, and is still a topic of contention. The shocking consequences of the rate established are apparent. What should be underlined is that, given the tremendous difference between the economies of the FRG and the GDR and the perceived need for their immediate union (including the overwhelming weight of noneconomic factors in shaping the unification) *no appropriate or "satisfying" conversion rate could have been established.* To put it simply, a lesser (than agreed-on) revaluation of the mark would have meant not only a better competitive position and less indebtedness vis-à-vis the state for East German enterprises but a much greater cut in assets, starting wages, and other incomes for the population. The federal government at the time was right in assuming that a more competitive conversion rate might have been politically unacceptable to the East German population. According to analysts, any advantages of a more competitive rate would have been reduced to nought by the inevitable sharp wage increases.[17] At the same time, neglect of the specifics of the East German economic situation and a lack of fine-tuning of the currency change added much to the unavoidable difficulties.

The other question is what the potential and actual benefits of the "big bang" will be for the eastern part of Germany. The unique feature of the East German situation is that because of the tremendous West German financial transfers, amounting to almost DM-100 billion in 1991 alone, Germany could "afford" the terrible decline in East German production and income. Moreover, the longer-term prospects for external financing of the East German economy are brighter than in the Five. It remains to be seen whether these significantly more favorable conditions will, as is officially expected, bring about a swifter recovery and a stronger restructuring and rise to European (or West German) industrial levels and living conditions than in the other former CMEA member countries. There are some very weighty factors on the negative side.

First, the GDR was one of the few socialist countries to have taken almost no steps toward creating the conditions for a market economy, and this may prove a serious obstacle to increasing efficiency in the wake of rapid marketization in some fields (i.e., large-scale heavy industries that have been oriented almost exclusively to the Soviet market) despite the introduction of the West German legal and economic systems. Second, the longer-term impacts of the present very serious decline in production are not yet clear and may be varied. For example, by eliminating uncompetitive and obsolete activities it may clear the way for healthy development but at the same time large-scale labor migration to West Germany may continue. Wages will continue to increase to match West German levels more rapidly than productivity, and therefore the position of East Germany as an investment location may remain questionable. Third and most important, not only has the East German national economy ceased to exist as a consequence of unification but the East German population is completely uninvolved in political and economic decision making concerning its own fate. A kind of West

German tutelage prevails concerning the important questions of life in East Germany, including economic restructuring.[18] Even if there are plausible explanations for this policy, it is doubtful whether a general upswing can be achieved without an active and creative involvement of the population.

Although it is West German financial support that makes shock therapy in East Germany manageable, the availability of West German assistance in itself is not an argument in favor of the "big bang." In principle, availability of assistance has not been restricted to the shock-therapy approach. Had political considerations allowed for gradualism in economic reunification, financial assistance could have come in similar forms and amounts.

The Case for Gradualism

The foregoing analysis suggests that where conditions permit, the governments of countries in transition should choose a gradual approach to reforming their economies instead of the messianism of shock therapy. Before turning to the experiences with a gradual approach to stabilization and liberalization in Central and Eastern Europe, two remarks are apposite. First, by any conventional economic standards, the pace of systemic change in the countries that have chosen a gradual approach is very dynamic. No more rapid systemic transition has been seen since the discontinuation of the market economy in the aftermath of the October Revolution in Soviet Russia and after the communist takeover in the late 1940s in Central and Eastern Europe. In addition, this gradual approach is being adopted in countries that have already been shocked by a decade-long economic decline followed by a severe recession. Second, as has already been indicated, gradualism is a philosophy proposing step-by-step changes as opposed to attempting to solve the difficult problems of transition at a single stroke. In the case of very serious disequilibria, gradualism implies a clear-cut distinction between stabilization and structural reform, timing and sequencing liberalization accordingly. Gradualism may in practice involve very different economic policies, ranging from consistent reform to evasion of reform. Therefore, our preference for gradualism does not imply any judgment about particular policies in the countries in which gradualism prevails.

In this context, it becomes obvious why it is difficult to draw a clear line between shock therapy and gradualism for systemic transformation in Central and Eastern Europe. A case in point is Czechoslovakia. As has frequently been pointed out both by Czechoslovakian economists and foreign observers (Hrnčíř 1991, Williamson 1991), the initial macroeconomic conditions for systemic transformation appeared at least in some respect more favorable here than in other countries of the region because of "traditionally prudent monetary, credit, fiscal, and income policies." Domestic macroeconomic stability and the level of foreign indebtedness were relatively satisfactory at the time of political change. At the same time, despite macroeconomic prudence and a long tradition of industrial development, Czechoslovakia's technological level, industrial patterns (the predominance of smokestack industry), the environment, and growth and export performance were mediocre to poor even by Central European standards. Beyond the predominant political conditions, an important reason for this situation was the traditional mandatory planning and resource allocation system that remained practically intact in Czechoslovakia until the very end of the ancien régime. Furthermore, discussions concerning the means and the desirable pace of transition in this country were protracted. This may explain why the old economic system essentially survived well into 1990.

As Hrnčíř (1991, p. 23) explains, after long discussions between proponents of "fast" and "slow" transition, the Czechoslovak government opted for "a *radical systems change and a transition path as quick as feasible*. At the same time, the measures adopted take into account the differentiated time scales of the various elements making up the transition process." In accordance with this approach, policy makers in Czechoslovakia seem to have been very critical of gradualism.

The introduction of the internal convertibility of the Czech kopina on 1 January 1991 (together with its strong devaluation, monetary austerity, and other measures) was much less drastic than the Polish shock therapy. Williamson (1991, p. 70) seems to be right in saying that the Czechoslovak program is close to a "minimum bang." Nevertheless, the economy has suffered severe shocks. In 1991 industrial production declined by 22 percent and GDP by 12–14 percent compared with the preceding year. As has been mentioned, real wages declined by more than 20 percent. Unemployment is on the rise—in Slovakia it is already more than 10 percent. Critically minded economists also emphasize that the decline in production and incomes involves "a structural downward trend, a rise in the share of primary heavy industries, in export, in production and in profits. . . . the already excessive, energetic and material consumption of our economy continues to rise by about 3 per cent per annum (although it was approximately about one half higher compared with the developed world)" (Pick 1991, p. 2). Although a large part of the 1991 difficulties must be attributed to the collapse of CMEA trade (see Chapter 4), it is clear that even managing a "minimum bang" can be a very complicated process. The general assumption is that 1992 will be a year of further significant economic decline (at least 5 percent of GDP) and further increase in unemployment. At the same time, both government and expert observers forecast an inflation rate of 10–15 percent, which might be a unique achievement in present-day Central and Eastern Europe.

Distinguishing the Czechoslovakian case (as a "minimum bang") from the shock therapy applied in Poland and elsewhere can be challenged given that, for instance, the Czechoslovakian government proudly declares that its policy is shock therapy and its critics focus on its mistakes in those terms (Komarek 1992). To be sure, the Czechoslovak adjustment program is less painful than the therapies applied elsewhere in Central and Eastern Europe. At the same time, it differs from other programs in that it was launched in a context of relative macroeconomic equilibrium (no significant inflation, no shortages, no unmanageable external debt)—that is, in a situation that apparently did not call for major *stabilization* surgery. Whereas in Poland and other countries some kind of surgery was unavoidable if there was to be meaningful structural reform, in Czechoslovakia surgery (involving rapid price liberalization, import liberalization labeled "internal convertibility," and budgetary and monetary austerity that led to sharp declines in domestic demand) was a policy *choice* presumably based largely on theoretical and political considerations. But because this *was* surgery (even if less serious than the Polish), designating the program "shock therapy" is also plausible.

Hungary is the only country of the Five in which a gradual approach to systemic transformation is generally considered appropriate. This consensus does not exclude deep divisions concerning other issues of economic policy or interpretations of the suggested content of a gradual approach. It simply expresses a disbelief in any "great leap forward" or single, well-constructed policy package that would enable the economy to rid itself once and for all of inherited economic burdens and handicaps and structural illnesses. It means suspicion of simplistic notions such as that convertibility of the domestic currency, price stabilization, and strong export initiatives are *sufficient* conditions for recovery and lasting economic growth (Köves and Oblath 1991). Gradual policies may of course end in shock therapy under certain circumstances, but the approach assumes, first, that it is preferable to avoid those circumstances and that this is precisely the aim of economic policy and, second, that shock therapy, even if it proves inevitable, will *not* solve the problems of establishing a market economy.

The differences in pretransformation economic systems and macroeconomic and political conditions that made shock therapy inevitable in Poland and gradualism possible and desirable in Hungary have already been mentioned. To return to one important point about the merits of gradualism as opposed to shock therapy, it is often argued, as Williamson mentions (1991, p. 71), that the lessons of the Hungarian economic reform "show the perils of gradualism: 23 years after a major reform was started, Hungary has still not achieved a market economy." A possible response to this is that "until 1987 the Hungarian political leadership had made no real commitment to reform and its policies amounted to a series of pragmatic changes undertaken in response to particular problems as they arose."[19] Whether Hungarian reforms in the period 1968–1989 were successful depends on the criteria one uses. That the failure to achieve a market economy before 1989 is proof of the weakness of the approach is not, however, empirically supported. It was, in the first place, undoubtedly international political constraints and not gradualism that prevented the creation of a market economy in Hungary. Moreover, the important changes in priorities in economic policy and domestic policy in general, and the emphasis on political opening, consumer satisfaction, and work incentives (largely outside the traditional framework of the state owned enterprises) made Hungary, with its developing commodity markets and embryonic labor markets, a nonmarket economy quite different from the traditional Soviet-type ones. To be sure, the Hungarian reform was not fully implemented and had ideological and political limitations, and many of its originally declared aims proved illusory (Kornai 1986). Indeed, few of the major innovations for changing the way a socialist economy functions produced the expected amount of positive effects. Perhaps the most notorious example is that because government and business could not be separated, abolishing mandatory planning and resource allocation resulted in a kind of nontraditional, indirect central planning and management in its stead.

The relevant question concerning the pre-1989 Hungarian reform is whether it eased the burden of economic transformation in Hungary after the political change. Is the Hungarian economy better suited to transition to a market economy as a consequence of twenty years of reform than it would have been without that reform? All of the available evidence (including comparisons with other economies in transition) suggests that the answer is yes. More important, that economic agents (the bureaucracy, managers, employees, consumers—the entire population) have had decades of experience with a more open and business-oriented system means that they have had a head start in the inevitably long learning process with regard to the organizational and legal systems, modes of operation, habits of thought, sociology and psychology, and international relations associated with market-type economic development. It is true that, in some very important respects (such as property rights), the Rubicon could only be crossed after political change, but the majority of the liberalizing reforms instituted in most other former socialist countries after 1989 had been progressing well in Hungary since the introduction of the "New Economic Mechanism" in 1968.

In spite of the relative advantages related to the long-standing economic reform, it would be premature to assert that Hungarian gradualism is guaranteed to succeed. Although decline in economic growth and incomes or in employment in Hungary is more modest and social conflicts are less intense and imbalances less acute than in most of Central and Eastern Europe, the economic crisis is protracted and significant by international standards and it is far from certain that it will soon be over. The reasons for this are multiple. For example, imprudent past macroeconomic policies bear a large share of responsibility for the huge foreign debt. The need to manage the debt and to overcome the recent external shocks (the collapse of Eastern trade) restrict the scope for macroeconomic policy action and make austerity inevitable.

Inflation clearly remains public enemy number one. Yet anti-inflationary policies must not disregard balance-of-payments targets as well as the deep recession (GDP declined by 4–6 percent in 1990 and 7–9 per cent in 1991). The serious (15 percent) 1991 decline in industrial production is also interpreted as a warning signal. Unemployment continues to increase much more rapidly than expected, and there is a severe decline in personal consumption (7-8 per cent in 1991). There is a built-in structural deficit in the state budget amounting to 4-5 percent of GDP and aggravated by the recession. The timing, sequencing, and fine-tuning of macroeconomic policy and liberalization measures require the utmost professional and political skill. Striking a balance between the need for prudent macroeconomic policies, on the one hand, and the avoidance of social strains and political conflict, on the other, is an extremely difficult task. The balancing act is complicated by inflationary pressures and the growing social conflict, over the politically charged issue of redistribution of state property among its prenationalization and precollectivization owners (traditional churches included), mostly at the expense of the lower strata of the population that are already threatened by inflation, unemployment, and cuts in social services. The role of the state (the scope as well as the form of government intervention) in the economy in general and in managing the processes of systemic transformation (including privatization) is subject to ongoing professional discussion and party politicking.

Notes

1. This statement certainly holds true from the very beginning of the new system for Poland, Czechoslovakia, and Hungary. Notwithstanding political difficulties and a chaotic economic situation, transformation to a market economy seems to have become the dominant strategy in Romania and Bulgaria as well. In the former Soviet Union it was only quite recently that establishing a Western-type market economy became the officially declared strategic aim of the ruling elites. At least until the defeat of the conservative coup in August 1991, the Soviet federal government continued to proclaim its adherence to socialism.

2. The existence of this "third-way" ideology and of populist groups *within* the new elites, however, leaves its mark on the behavior of the new governments and parliaments. It would be difficult to suppose, after more than forty years of planned economies in Central and Eastern Europe, that advocates of the Soviet type system had entirely disappeared, but they remain very limited in numbers (as in many countries they have been for years) and outside the political and professional elites.

3. "The winners of the day are those who promise to shorten the transition to a prosperous market economy, even at the price of a significant drop in economic activities, in the standard of living and in employment levels during the period of transition. Those who advocate a more reasoned gradual approach to the manifold steps of transformation are immediately labelled as conservative, as unwilling to hand over the old bureaucratic controls and on the whole as hindering the transition to a market economy" (Levcik, 1991, p. 1).

4. As Dornbusch argues, gradualism is largely illusion: " . . . The administrative capacity for successful gradual reform simply does not exist. After all, communism— even with the advantage of repression—could not handle the task of allocating resources reasonably efficiently. . . . In the grey area between a control economy that no longer functions and a market economy that is not fully accepted, economic collapse is inevitable" (1991, p. 171). This is a very pessimistic assessment both for the countries that

Shock Therapy Versus Gradual Change

have chosen gradualism and for those that have not been able to leap far enough to reach the heavens of the full-fledged market economy "in seven days." Actually, the Soviet Union is so far the only country to which this harsh verdict surely applies, and even in this case the political collapse is in large part responsible for the economic one.

5. There are other ways of listing the areas of necessary policy action in economies in transition. Some observers insist that the creation of other institutions of a market economy, such as a system of financial intermediation capable of managing the whole process of privatization and liberalization, is as important as other measures of systemic transformation and should precede them (Brainard, 1991).

6. These reformist tasks for economies in transition are of course associated with political change in Central and Eastern Europe, but it should not be forgotten that action on *all these fronts*, although weak, inconclusive, contradictory, and consequently to a large extent unsuccessful, began earlier in some of the Five. The clearest case is macroeconomic stabilization that was a priority policy task in Romania, Poland, and Hungary throughout the 1980s. Economic reforms aimed at moving away from traditional central planning and toward the development of market relations were steps, however inconsistent, toward economic liberalization. It is true that the overwhelming state ownership of the means of production was nowhere questioned until the very end of the ancien régime. Yet, for good or bad, important changes concerning property rights did take place in some countries. For example, in Poland and Hungary enterprise councils were established and received some property rights with regard to their enterprises. In Hungary, commercialization of state enterprises preceded political change. More important, development of the small-scale private sector, legal and semilegal, commenced in Hungary more than a decade ago. In Polish agriculture a private sector, though very weak, has survived four decades of central planning.

7. For the classical explanation, see Kornai (1980); for an account of the pre-1990 Polish shortage economy, see Lipton and Sachs (1990b).

8. In arguing for rapid transition, David Lipton and Jeffrey Sachs refer to Machiavelli's famous advice that a government should bring all of the bad news forward (1990b).

9. This paragraph draws heavily on Rosati (1990 and 1991).

10. It is another matter that, according to Kolodko (1991, pp. 14–15), the hyperinflation of late 1989 was to a large extent induced—a political choice "of using inflation to curb inflation" that was partially "encouraged by the practical situation, especially the coincidence of a change of government and outbreak of rampant inflationary processes."

11. For a more detailed account of the Polish debt renegotiations, see Chapter 7.

12. Sharp devaluation may also have contributed to the government's inability to contain inflation (Oblath 1991a).

13. This paragraph follows KOPINT-DATORG (1991a).

14. This paragraph draws heavily on Oblath (1991b).

15. For an account of the different concepts of convertibility, see Köves and Marer (1991b).

16. Because there had been no single exchange rate for the domestic currency in the GDR, it is difficult to quantify the revaluation. However, the fact that East German enterprises had been exporting to the West at an average exchange rate of 4:1 (in electronics, the rate was 4.8:1) provides some idea of its order of magnitude.

17. As Williamson (1991, p. 65) puts it, "wages in eastern Germany rose briskly after unification, so it seems rather doubtful that a more competitive initial exchange rate

would have done anything much except reduce the stock of assets held by East Germans after union."

18. To quote an American sociologist explaining the situation, "together with an abiding trust in the market, this political leadership [the German government] has a *profound trust in the state*. This trust, moreover, is accompanied by a deep, and almost indiscriminate, *distrust of East German society* (both italics in the original). Forty years of communism, according to German leadership, have produced a terrible human tragedy— the personality structures, habits, dispositions, expectations, and mentalities of the citizens of the new lands make them unfit and incapable of managing their affairs. It is not their fault, but they are no longer trustworthy. They must be remolded and re-educated not simply in industrial skills but with new mentalities" (Stark 1991, p. 42).

19. Williamson (1991, p. 71) notes: "Interestingly, these piecemeal reforms do not seem to have led to the type of second-best difficulties experienced by other countries introducing partial reforms. This provides perhaps the best evidence that a feasible sequence of partial reforms does exist." He concludes (p. 73): "The main lesson of the Hungarian experience seems to be that gradualism does not deserve the contemptuous dismissal that it has tended to receive in much recent discussion. Under certain circumstances it does provide a feasible road to reform. But this is surely true only where the economy has never been allowed to get out of hand, which excludes a gradualist strategy for most of the countries of the region."

2

Dilemmas of Privatization

The reform of property rights is the cornerstone of systemic transformation from Soviet-type central planning to a market economy. It was clear from the outset that the discontinuation of state ownership of most property,[1] the privatization of state-owned enterprises, and the establishment of a viable private sector in the economy could not be accomplished overnight (not even shock treatment can produce private entrepreneurs and enterprises). Rapid privatization is frequently regarded as the top priority and a prerequisite for successful transition.

Arguments for Rapid Privatization: A Brief Overview and Assessment

Arguments in favor of rapid privatization emphasize the inherent inefficiencies of the state-owned sector as impediments to macroeconomic stabilization and liberalizing reforms in Central and Eastern Europe. Such policies will need to be supported, it is argued, by the swift emergence of a strong private sector. "Until privatization has been accomplished, the economic crisis is likely to persist" (Aslund 1991, p. 30). Aslund suggests that privatization will solve all the problems of transformation and lead to robust economic growth. He anticipates growth rates on the order of 8 percent a year, given that the Five "are latecomers in terms of economic development with low labor costs but basically relatively skilled labor on the verge of the biggest market in the world—the European free trade area of the EC and EFTA [European Free Trade Association]" (Aslund 1991, p. 22).

Various factors are stressed in explaining why slower privatization has a negative impact on economic prospects. Aslund adds, for example, that "privatization is a precondition of a breakthrough of competent managers." Another factor, according to the *Economist* (11 May 1991), is inflation fueled by the absence of financial discipline for managers of state-owned firms and by expanding forced interenterprise credit. "As the competitive squeeze on enterprises tightens, the coming debt crunch will only grow—unless capital is quickly transferred to owners with reason to preserve its value. . . . the government is unlikely to be able to enforce financial discipline if state-owned enterprises remain a dominant part of the economy" (Blommestein, Marrese, and Zecchini 1991, p. 12). Sachs (1991b, pp. 161, 170) suggests that with protracted privatization "governments will be weighed down for years and years with specific problems of specific enterprises" instead of reforming and restructuring their economies. He maintains that upward pressure on wages is inherent in the preprivatization situation and that the notion that government-controlled enterprises can function efficiently "is a myth." A final factor is that there is no time to "put enterprises in shape" before privatization.

A Hungarian study (Horváth 1991) refers to Kornai's theory (1990b) of the affinity between state ownership and bureaucratic coordination, on the one hand, and private ownership and market coordination, on the other.[2] Horváth argues that, as a consequence, state ownership will remain dominant following the collapse of communist regimes, and the mechanisms that feed the overwhelmingly bureaucratic coordination of the economy will also persist. Therefore rapid privatization is needed to cut the umbilical cord between political power and the economy.

Lastly, there are arguments based on the undesirability of a protracted transitional period that would create uncertainty for economic agents. Most important, it is suggested that until "full" or predominant privatization has been achieved, the remaining state-owned enterprises will experience a sense of insecurity that will discourage any rational restructuring or investment policy.

In our opinion, however, some of these arguments tend to oversimplify both the state of affairs in present-day Central and Eastern Europe and the consequences of policies aimed at rapid as opposed to slower privatization. No question about the inherent inefficiencies of state-owned enterprises, but the *specific* shortcomings of state enterprises *in Central and Eastern Europe* were a function of one-party rule, central planning, and economic autarky. It is simply unrealistic to ignore the impact of political change and ongoing economic transformation on organizational and behavioral patterns in state-owned enterprises. It is worth reviewing the most important developments: elimination of central planning and of the monopolistic positions of large state enterprises in domestic markets; import liberalization; the end of the CMEA and state trading (coupled with the collapse of their most important Soviet export market); the perceived need for export reorientation; cuts in government subsidies; the introduction of new, very complicated relationships between state-owned enterprises and governments; the end of the shortage economy; and, finally, restrictive monetary policies. In most countries these and other changes in the economic and political environment have inevitably affected the way in which state-owned enterprises function. What is more, an increasing proportion of state-owned enterprises is already being commercialized—reorganized into joint stock or limited liability companies (this reorganization occasionally involving the breakup of monopolies). The process of commercialization is highly controversial and fiercely debated (Móra 1990). What is now emerging in place of traditional "socialist" enterprises with well-analyzed structures and behavioral patterns is a plethora of different ownership forms and combinations of shareholders (state, banks, other creditors, partners, and employees). As a result, sweeping generalizations concerning the behavioral patterns of state-owned enterprises and their managers in Central and Eastern Europe are now subject to question. Indeed, commercialization makes state-owned enterprises institutionally capable of incorporating private (foreign) investment (KOPINT-DATORG 1991b), and therefore privatization typically involves only the sale of some of their shares. The earlier clear-cut line between the (overwhelmingly dominant) state sector and the private one in Central and Eastern Europe is fading. It is true that change in enterprise behavior is slow and inconsistent and that significant intercountry differences remain. It would be premature to speak of any fundamental break with the past. The tremendous legal and institutional uncertainties facing state-owned companies in fact compel them to adopt defensive and short-term strategies, and these behavioral patterns contribute to inflationary pressures and the interenterprise debt crisis. Yet in view of rapidly declining real wages in all of the countries of the region, it would be inappropriate to regard the average current wage increases in the state-owned sector as excessive. Moreover, the private sector's having much higher wages has a demonstration effect that contributes to wage inflation. According to the most recent Hungarian research, there is no evidence to suggest that progress in privatization alone would lead to disinflation (Petschnig and Voszka 1991).

Enterprise debt is rightly regarded as one of the most difficult present-day economic problems in many Central and East European countries. It is not easy to answer the question whether privatization per se might be a solution to the enterprise debt crisis. (We will return to this problem later.) Inefficient management is also an inherited problem rooted in the economic and political environment in which state-owned enterprises long had to exist. The quality of management has of course tended to adapt to changes in the political situation and economic policies of the respective regimes. As political and economic liberalization has progressed, the management of a growing number of state-owned enterprises has become more business-oriented. Of greater significance, "there is no alternative managerial elite waiting in the wings to take over from the incumbents" (Dhanji and Milanovic 1991, p. 19). It is unreasonable to expect that privatization by itself will produce capitalist-type managers.

In sum, there is no theoretical or empirical evidence to suggest that rapid privatization will lead to a rapid transformation of state-owned enterprises. The process of change will be difficult and protracted under any scheme of privatization these governments might be willing to undertake. In turn, an early start in the process of transformation (within the framework of state ownership) may contribute to making privatization easier.

Privatization from a Broader Perspective

Most of the above arguments and counterarguments concerning privatization are related to the restructuring of state-owned enterprises. In fact, systemic transformation from the point of view of property rights means more than privatization of what the state once owned. There are two parallel processes that can lead to discontinuation of the predominance of state (and so-called collective) ownership in Central and Eastern Europe: the privatization of the state-owned sector and the development of new, initially small-scale private firms. Theoretically at least (and consistent with the experiences of some developing countries), the latter process by itself may lead to the predominance of private enterprise even if it is not accompanied by complete privatization of the state-owned sector. For example, this has been the experience in Taiwan.[3] The process, though undoubtedly slower than that based on change in ownership of the state-owned sector, may be dynamic as well if it is supported by an influx of foreign investment, liberalization of the economy, and government policies promoting entrepreneurship. This has not been discussed as a possible strategy for further economic development by any of the Five. In Central and Eastern Europe the predominant state-owned sector of the economy was identified with the communist regime of central planning, and this may explain why the notion of systemic transformation in all of its interpretations involved large-scale privatization of state-owned industries.[4] Nevertheless, at different rates and in the face of a great many practical difficulties—legal, financial, infrastructural, and so on—the development of the new private sector has begun or is continuing throughout the region.

In Central and Eastern Europe the privatization of the state-owned sector involves an accepted distinction between "small" and "large" privatization. The first means selling to the public retail shops, restaurants, and other service establishments that, in most cases, had been units of larger state-owned trading or servicing chains. Once again, schemes of small privatization in different countries have had varied success.[5] By all accounts, small-scale privatization is very important in Central and Eastern Europe today. Stanley Fischer of the Massachusetts Institute of Technology, former vice president of the World Bank and a partisan of rapid privatization of the state-owned sector remarks that

> the key to the long-run transformation of the FSEs [former socialist economies] may be less in the privatization of the very large industrial firms . . . than in the development of new firms and the growth of existing smaller firms. For that reason, rapid progress in other areas, such as the creation of a suitable legal environment, price decontrol, industrial deregulation, and trade liberalization, is as important to the development of a vibrant private sector as privatization of large firms (1991, p. 25).

"Large" privatization is one of the most fiercely debated issues of systemic transformation.[6] What follows is not a systematic overview of the issues involved but rather a focus on some strategic problems of privatization that are important mostly from the point of view of the rapidity of the transformation. The experience of the past two years in Central and Eastern Europe suggests that privatization of state-owned enterprises is a much more difficult undertaking than was once perceived. As strange as it may seem, the greatest difficulties have been encountered in the countries with the strongest belief in the need for privatization. This phenomenon is explained by the enormous difficulties, technical as well as theoretical, of devising feasible schemes for overnight privatization. Some of these difficulties are the following: First, the evidence suggests that the economic conditions of the Five preclude rapid application of the "normal" commercial methods of case-by-case privatization; what is called "rapid" privatization can be achieved only through artificial schemes of *giving away* state property.[7] Second, giveaway schemes are technically far too complicated and of dubious effect. Third, in contrast to the arguments for the establishment of a viable private sector (partly based on the traditional state-owned enterprises) as the substance of systemic transformation in Central and Eastern Europe, theories stressing accelerated privatization are essentially flawed and unconvincing and may effectively delay stabilization and recovery.

Some Principal Difficulties of Privatization

The predominance of state ownership in Central and Eastern Europe has meant a complete absence of legal and institutional foundations for privatization. First, because of the obscurity of state ownership (everybody's property is no one's property), the most difficult issue of all is determining *who* (government, enterprises, local governments) can sell *what* property under *what* conditions. These questions are largely responsible for the length of time it takes to develop privatization schemes and the intricacy of the practical privatization process (these issues cannot be regarded as settled in any country of Central and Eastern Europe).[8] Secondly, legal regulation is also necessary concerning to whom and according to what criteria state property can be sold (or given away). This is a tremendously difficult political as well as legal problem; many of the institutions that are supposed to play a significant role as would-be owners of state property (pension funds, holding companies, mutual funds, commercial and specialized banks, and other financial institutions) have in most cases been established simultaneously with or subsequent to the legislation concerning privatization. Following policy deliberations concerning the role of foreign capital (in the economy in general and in the privatization process in particular), foreign investment laws were to be reconsidered and improved in all countries. Third, the scope of privatization of state-owned enterprises (what should be privatized and according to what criteria) has yet to be determined. There is a need for sectoral privatization policies, for example, concerning agriculture, and for policies concerning specific types of property such as land or housing. Fourthly, progress on privatization has been hampered by attempts at *reprivatization* and *compensation* of former owners for lost property. Clearly, both sellers and potential buyers of state property are being discouraged from committing themselves to specific agreements before property rights have been determined. As a matter of fact, all of the Five have engaged in partial and limited reprivatization, but the whole legal issue is far from being closed, and controversies concerning what belongs to whom may continue well into the years to come.

This is the legal and institutional background of the political and social difficulties of privatization. Each of these issues concerns a vested interest. Legislation and policy decisions generally reflect the outcome of keen struggles between government and opposition, between state bureaucracy and enterprise managers, between employers and employees, or within the government itself. These circumstances add to the economic difficulties of systemic transformation.

The most vigorous policy discussion concerning the case-by-case privatization of state-owned enterprises relates to centralization vs. decentralization. Obviously, centralization of decision making gives government tremendous power in shaping the privatization process according to its own economic philosophy. Considerations of party politics and other biases override business-type considerations specific to the enterprises involved. Of all the former socialist countries, East Germany has the most centralized process of privatization under its Treuhandanstalt (State Property Agency). Though subject to policy changes, centralization has also been strong in Hungary in 1990–1991. Where privatization is decentralized ("spontaneous"), enterprise-specific considerations and the interests of management are being honored. However, because of the absence of effective control, fairness across transactions cannot be taken for granted, and the government budget and other macroeconomic considerations may suffer as a consequence (sharp criticism has led to revision of the procedures for spontaneous privatization). A specific concern is that, in the process, state-owned enterprises may use up a considerable part of the state property, as in effect they can do in selling property units. To avoid this impasse, the Hungarian policy discussions produced the idea of "privatization of privatization," a sort of continuation of "privatization from below" (i.e., privatizations initiated by enterprises themselves). The idea that seems to have gained ground in late 1991 is that once rules and regulations for the privatization of state-owned enterprises are firmly established, independent (domestic or foreign) firms should conduct the procedures of privatization according to business principles and be free from government intervention. Although this is a good idea, arriving at unbiased decisions based on high professional standards will remain very difficult. Nevertheless, establishing clear-cut economic norms and a legal and institutional framework for privatization and eliminating political uncertainties with regard to property rights should be the first priority for the governments of the Five. This kind of commitment could help smooth the progress of privatization.

There are in addition serious economic problems that militate against a rush toward privatization. On the one hand, the potential domestic demand for state-owned property is clearly insufficient to support rapid privatization in any country.[9] Therefore, there is a tremendous need for foreign investment in Central and Eastern Europe. It is no overstatement to say that the fate of privatization, and especially its pace, in these countries is to a very large degree dependent on the inflow of Western capital. Chapter 3 will be primarily devoted to the problems and prospects for foreign direct investment in Central and Eastern Europe. Suffice it to say that we do *not* see any particular reason that foreign capital could not play a very significant role in the privatization process. With some exceptions, however, capital inflow has scarcely begun, and often the same factors that hinder privatization also prevent a surge of Western investment.

There are major obstacles in the bargaining process[10] and on the supply side of privatization. With regard to the latter, one of these is the condition of the state-owned industries; their technological level, production structure, organization, management skills and marketing pattern often add up to low efficiency levels. The generally accepted pattern in market economies of upgrading individual state-owned *enterprises* by bold financing and restructuring before privatization clearly do not apply in the case of the full-scale (or large-scale) privatization of *economies*. In this context, it is true that the desirability of upgrading in itself cannot be considered an argument for delaying privatization. At the same time, the privatization of inefficient, failing, and indebted enterprises is especially problematic. For obvious reasons, the new owners tend to opt for the rapid elimination of unprofitable activities, and political opposition to this may be acute because of the fear of layoffs and unemployment. The problem, however, is that the elimination of unprofitable activities represents but the initial phase of enterprise restructuring. From a macroeconomic point of view, the question is whether this "negative" restructuring will *as a rule* be followed by a positive one. Without investment in new profitable activities and/or in making existing ones efficient, privatization will only exacerbate the economic crisis.[11] Considerations of the interrelationship between privatization (and other marketing reforms) and the current economic performance of countries undergoing transition should be highlighted in examining the pros and cons of different policies.

Giveaway Privatization: How and Why?

Giveaway schemes for privatization have emerged in Central and Eastern Europe as a response to the economic and other difficulties of the case-by-case sale of state-owned enterprise. According to these schemes, giving shares of a large proportion of state-owned enterprises to the public is the main technique of privatization. Some form of giveaway or sale under highly favorable terms is found in all of the privatization plans of Central and Eastern Europe,[12] and in most cases it may be regarded as a complementary to case-by-case privatization. What we are concerned with here is giveaway privatization that substitutes for the sale of state-owned enterprises.

Arguments for the giveaway approach involve principles such as fairness and social justice, but presumably these schemes came into being for other reasons—namely, the lack of domestic capital to fuel privatization demand, aggravated by the difficulties of foreign investment. Czechoslovakia and Poland, the two countries in which giveaway privatization schemes have emerged, are characterized not only by reservations on the part of potential foreign investors (which are general in Central and Eastern Europe) but also domestic ambivalence toward foreign investment. This partly explains why the potential income from the sale of shares in state-owned enterprises is not considered one of the important aims of privatization. The respective governments have apparently accepted the need for rapid and decisive action on privatization—an idea in accordance with their overall philosophy concerning the pace of systemic transformation (see Chapter 1). In addition, it may well be that lack of experience in the gradual restructuring of enterprises (an important part of the long reform process in Hungary) has led these governments to doubt the feasibility of case-by-case restructuring of enterprises.

In Czechoslovakia massive privatization through vouchers began late in 1991, and its first phase, involving a transfer of up to 20 percent of the book value of the property of state-owned enterprises, is scheduled to be completed by mid-1992. The realization of the Polish scheme, developed under previous governments, is uncertain. In fact, the two schemes are conceptually different, the single similarity between them being that both use vouchers.[13] In the Polish scheme vouchers are freely distributed as a portion of the "national patrimony" to all 27 million adult citizens of the country. Individuals are not supposed to use their vouchers to buy shares in formerly state-owned enterprises; instead they are expected to put them into one of several "investment funds" that are to be established. As the *Economist* (11 May 1991) comments, the expectation is that these funds "will act as an investment bank, mutual fund, venture-capital manager, auditor, and consulting firm all rolled into one." Initially, majority ownership of four hundred state-owned firms, representing 25 percent of industrial sales, will be allocated to voucher-holding funds. Individual voucher-holders will be able to trade their shares in the investment fund after a period yet to be determined. The funds will own 60 percent of company shares; 30 percent of shares will be state-owned and 10 percent owned by the employees.

It is clear that it will take many years for this scheme to lead to a system in which individual citizens are *company* shareholders. This may or may not be necessary, but the question is whether an investment fund owned(?) by millions of individuals could in fact act as a more efficient owner of the currently state-owned enterprises than a state agency or a state-owned holding company. Does the scheme *really* mean privatization of state-owned assets, or is it rather a kind of restructuring of central management of state enterprises, with investment funds replacing industrial ministries? There are no satisfactory answers to these questions.

According to the Czechoslovak scheme, vouchers are offered to all adult citizens for a nominal sum and are to be used for purchasing shares of firms scheduled to be privatized. Citizens have to pay to register their vouchers, and these are not regarded as national patrimony. "Those participating [in the auctions] will be risking something and so will take an immediate interest in the shares they receive," according to the *Economist*. In Czechoslovakia, in contrast to Poland, shares in the firms, not in investment funds, will be auctioned. Investment funds will, however, play an important role in auctions in that individual citizens may sell their vouchers to such funds. In this case, citizens will become shareholders of funds rather than firms. It seems a complicated task to ensure that all participants in these auctions have equal access to the information about the state-owned enterprises subject to auction that will allow them to choose among a wide range of investment opportunities. But in the absence of this access not only will equality and fairness suffer but expectations concerning risk-taking and entrepreneurial behavior on the part of shareholders may prove illusory.[14]

Is It Really Speed That Counts?

The above brief overview of emerging schemes for rapid privatization and their difficuties leads us to some pertinent conclusions. The fundamental problem of economic transition is that privatization as one of its major objectives probably *cannot* be artificially accelerated in any rational manner. Schemes that aim to privatize by parceling out state property within a short period of time cannot be implemented, partly for technical reasons. In addition, the mass of small property owners that is created by this distribution scheme will hardly result in more efficient use of former state property. The genuineness of privatization by large-scale free disbursement of assets is in fact debatable. What is really needed first is the development of an administrative, legal, and political framework for the transfer of property to private hands. Excessive emphasis on speed is unwise in that it may produce economically (and probably politically) unmanageable solutions.

It follows from this that the transition to a market economy will take many years. In the absence of the international and domestic conditions that would permit a return to the old system, the rapidity of the transition cannot be the sole criterion for its success and must be assessed in the context of the current economic performance of the country in question. The solid arguments in favor of reducing the prevalence of state ownership and shifting to a market economy with a strong private sector do not imply that privatization of state-owned enterprises in Central and Eastern Europe, *irrespective of the form it takes,* leads to improved efficiency and performance. What is more, there is a serious danger that, under certain circumstances, ill-prepared and hasty privatization may lead to deterioration not only in the performance of the enterprises concerned but also in the macroeconomic situation and will effectively block consideration of the most important issues, such as putting a brake on the recession and the decline of living standards.

Fundamental to the transition to a market economy is the transformation of the state's economic role and property and management relations. This transformation must above all ensure the alteration of the structure of production and exports in accordance with world market standards. The abolition of outdated structures is a painful process and is itself a factor in the current deep recession, for these structures were capable only of producing goods for the CMEA and the domestic market and were supported by large state subsidies. However, no positive correlation can be demonstrated between the depth of the recession and the progress of economic transformation in the former socialist countries. The recession is at its most severe where only the negative part of the change of regime—the destruction of the old—is observable and there are as yet no plans for the construction of the new market system. The comprehensive development of market relations should bring the recession and the decline of living standards under control, especially because the market economy envisioned is similar to that in Western Europe, that is, based on the institutions of "social" and political democracy. The point here is that there are limits to what a society can bear, and violating these limits might have sociopolitical consequences that would thwart the whole economic policy and preclude (democratic) management of the crisis. As has already been mentioned, however, the basic aim of the transition to a market economy is efficient economic growth. With the preconditions for this clearly lacking in the present, difficult years of transition, the unexpectedly severe recession, the decline in living standards, and the widespread social disintegration could call into question the very meaning of systemic change.

Notes

1. It is estimated that the state owns 70–90 percent of the property in present-day Central and Eastern Europe.

2. Kornai himself is not a partisan of the rapid privatization of state-owned enterprises.

3. I owe this point to Gábor Oblath.

4. As Nuti (1991, pp. 52–53) explains, the drive toward privatization (which is not confined to Central and Eastern Europe) rests on the expectation that "privatization can raise efficiency through changed incentives." Arguments for privatization based on theories of the principal-agent relationship "may have to be modified. Public enterprises sometimes can be more efficient than their private counterparts . . . Privatization of management might achieve the same effects as privatization of ownership without divesting the state of its assets (i.e., the state could hold assets in private companies) . . . In the case of transitional economies, however, privatization not only raises the share of national assets held by private owners, it also extends the scope of ownership rights from absent or limited ownership to full-fledged private ownership. This qualitative aspect of privatization in transitional economies provides additional system-specific supportive arguments."

5. In Czechoslovakia, for example, small privatization means two-year leases on the shops and restaurants concerned. In Hungary schemes of small privatization have been unsuccessful so far. Among the reasons for the failure is that in most cases it is only rights to *lease* the shops that have been privatized (because the premises of the shops were owned by communal real-estate-managment enterprises) and would-be buyers were discouraged by the uncertainties involved in this scheme. The important point is that small privatization competes with the independent development of new private activities, which seem to be growing more successfully in Hungary—in themselves giving private-sector development a certain dynamism.

6. Some of the important English-language contributions are Blommestein and Marrese (1991), Dhanji and Milanovic (1991), Kornai (1990), Lipton and Sachs (1990), Stark (1991), and Tardos (1989). For an overview of questions of large privatization, see ECE (1991b).

7. Although it should be underlined once more that the pace of privatization in countries with gradualist policies may prove very rapid by international standards. For example, the Hungarian government plans to reduce the proportion of state property in the economy to less than 50 percent by 1994. Taking into account that what is involved here is, for all practical purposes, a total restructuring of the country's economy (and society), the target is overambitious rather than unduly circumspect and moderate.

8. For a comprehensive review of problems making divestiture of enterprises "considerably more complicated" for economies in transition than for others, see Dhanji and Milanovic (1991).

9. For example, according to estimates by the joint Hungarian-international Blue Ribbon Commission (1990, p. 26), the book value of all Hungarian state-owned enterprises in 1990 was about Ft2,000 billion (about $30 billion), while the current annual flow of private currency savings that might be available for purchasing assets (other than real estate) was not more than Ft20 billion (about $300 million) a year. What is more, though differences in origin within the private sector (whether "new" or privatized) will presumably fade with the passage of time, most private savings will probably be invested in activities other than large-privatized state-owned companies.

10. For example, "policy-makers and the public in former CPEs [centrally planned economies] do not possess a clear idea how capital markets operate," and "there are difficulties in establishing reservation prices (prices below which the state should not sell) since enterprises have not functioned in a market economy, have not faced serious competitive pressure and have not been audited in an economically meaningful manner" (Blommestein, Marrese, and Zecchini 1991, p. 13). It follows that the bargaining position of the seller (as against a foreign investor) is usually very weak. Additional causes of vulnerability are the weakness of the concept of state property and the perceived urgency of the privatization process. There is considerable anecdotal evidence of unrealistically low selling prices for state enterprises and other assets. This situation, in turn, has aroused public protest against "selling out" that has had the effect of slowing the process and inspiring a reconsideration of privatization schemes.

11. Clearly, the widespread Hungarian practice of breaking up state-owned enterprises and then selling the more efficient units to private owners while retaining the inefficient ones in state ownership (the latter in many cases "inheriting" most of the enterprises' preexisting debts) is also no solution.

12. For example, in Hungary shares in privatized (or even commercialized) compa-

nies are being sold *internally,* to workers and managers, on preferential terms. Local governments and pension funds are also being given shares freely. Finally, compensation of prenationalization owners with notes that can be used to buy shares in state-owned companies, as practiced in some countries, is also a kind of giveaway.

13. Other kinds of giveaway concepts seem to be emerging in some post-Soviet privatization plans. According to the Romanian privatization law passed in August 1991, 30 percent of state-owned property, approximately six thousand enterprises, is to be sold to five property-managing holding companies beginning in April 1992, and the properties of these holding companies will be freely distributed to the adult population. The remaining 70 percent will be retained in the state property fund and later privatized gradually on a case-by-case basis.

14. Privatization by vouchers in Czechoslovakia is related to central assessment of so-called enterprise privatization projects (prepared by the enterprises) and a central decision about the future distribution of enterprise shares (involving what proportion of the total shares will be distributed according to the voucher scheme). According to Pick (1991, p. 8), the price is an almost absurd, uncontrollable bureaucratization: "a central decision should be made concerning approx. 3.6 thousand privatization projects (based on the so-called entrepreneurial strategy) of individual enterprises. Never in the history of Czecho-Slovak central planning did the center decide about the future of thousands of individual enterprises (for that purpose it had a hierarchical pyramid of institutions—now abolished)—especially in such a short time span."

3

Systemic Transformation and Foreign Economic Liberalization: Trade and Investment Issues

One of the important conclusions of the previous chapter is that progress in privatization in Central and Eastern Europe is contingent upon foreign direct investment. This investment, influenced by the ongoing reforms, also plays an outstanding role in promoting economic liberalization and stabilization. From a broader perspective, the development of foreign economic relations, including trade, finance, and investment, is instrumental to systemic transformation in Central and Eastern Europe. Liberalizing reform in the fields of trade and investment is important in the industrializing and modernizing economies as well, but in Central and Eastern Europe some specific factors make it especially so.

First, aspiration to autarky (isolation from the international economy) was one of the most influential attributes of the Soviet-type planned economy, both for political reasons and because of the inherent logic of the economic system. Development strategies aimed at the highest possible level of self-sufficiency resulted in a degree of economic isolationism and institutional closedness probably unmatched by even the most inward-oriented of developing countries. The Central and East European countries had adopted a two-level autarky, one national and the other regional (CMEA) in scale. These levels functioned well together, as "cooperation within the CMEA was the alternative to organic participation in the single world economy not to national isolation" (Köves 1985, p. 137). There are two equally important points to be stressed concerning this two-level autarky. On the one hand, as strange as it may seem to an outside observer, the national economies of CMEA member countries were more—not less—institutionally isolated from each other than from countries outside the CMEA. It was the notorious state trading within the CMEA (see Chapter 4) that prompted this isolation. On the other, regional-level autarky was born out of the political divisions of the world. Central and East European dependence on the Soviet Union made the segregation of CMEA countries unique and especially severe. Foreign trade and investment regimes had served to separate the domestic from the international economy. Foreign investment was prohibited well into the 1970s or, in some cases, the 1980s.[1] It is no accident that changing the foreign trade regime was an important aspect of reformist thinking in Central and Eastern Europe from the very beginning. It is also clear why entering into the international economy is regarded as both an aim of and a prerequisite for the Five's economic transition.

Furthermore, the need to enter into the mainstream of the international economy is the more pressing because the Five are small or medium-sized economies that depend heavily on foreign trade. The high degree of import and export dependence renders autarkic policies in these countries especially inefficient and self-destructive.

Finally, the need for liberalization is very strong because the region's most difficult economic problems lie in the field of foreign economic relations. As has earlier been indicated, the hard currency indebtedness of the Five (with the possible exception of Czechoslovakia) is one of the crucial factors underlying economic policies of austerity. Foreign debt accumulation is in turn explainable in terms of the long-term consequences of attempts at autarky. Policies aimed at self-sufficiency are principally responsible for the export weakness of all of the former CMEA countries—the single most important reason for the cumulative trade imbalances that have led to increasing indebtedness.

As was pointed out in Chapter 1, the timing and sequencing of liberalization are at the forefront of controversies over economic transition. Foreign economic liberalization in Central and Eastern Europe includes restructuring of the relations with the former CMEA, liberalization of imports and exports, promotion of foreign direct investment, and steps in the direction of currency convertibility.[2] This chapter will briefly discuss some issues of trade liberalization and then review some of the most common problems of foreign investment.

Trade Liberalization in Practice

The arguments for instant convertibility vs. gradual foreign economic liberalization (including reform of trade regimes) have already been discussed, and although our preference for gradualism was made unequivocal it should be underlined that a gradual approach alone is no guarantee of success. Whether trade liberalization survives in the long run depends on various factors *outside* the scope of foreign trade regimes proper. According to international empirical evidence, it is balance-of-payments difficulties that are most often responsible for policy reversals. A deterioration of the balance of payments may be caused by external factors (international financial developments, price fluctuations in the world market, or, as now in the case of Central and Eastern Europe, collapse of trade with important partners, notably the Soviet Union), and domestic economic or political instability is also significant. However, both international experience and the recent Hungarian example suggest that the design of trade liberalization is of decisive importance.

The Hungarian scheme of abolishing the bulk of administrative controls (explicit and—mostly—implicit quotas) on imports in three years (1989–1991) is by international standards a very bold one.[3] A lack of well-designed industrial policies capable of determining which industries were in need of temporary protection and for how long made the sequencing of import liberalization somewhat ambiguous. Next, in contrast to the practice of many other countries, the abolition of quotas was not accompanied by attempts at the "tariffication" of protection. On the contrary, the Hungarian government, in negotiations within the General Agreement on Tariffs and Trade (GATT) framework, committed itself to tariff cuts parallel with the elimination of administrative restrictions on imports. The exchange-rate policy requirements of the liberalization scheme were also obscure. It was implied that no real and significant devaluation of the currency would be required for the liberalization policy to succeed. Because of the unexpected strong inflationary pressures in 1990 and 1991, however, the exchange-rate policies of those years were accompanied by strong anti-inflationary policies. Following the first two years, in which, to the surprise of critically minded Hungarian economists, liberalization progressed smoothly, some domestic industries affected by the surge in imports began to call for help. Given the 15 percent decline in industrial production in 1991, implying much deeper cuts in output in many branches of industry, the reasons for protectionist sentiments are obvious.

In 1991, balance-of-payments forecasts were within the targets agreed on by the Hungarian government and the IMF, but future difficulties cannot be ruled out. Because of the uncertainties involved, what is indispensable in this situation is not a rush toward convertibility[4] but a moderate policy that defends the current level of liberalization. This is a challenge for monetary and budgetary policy and for the development of domestic markets. Although not as grand a design, it is nevertheless a necessary condition for transition.[5]

An issue frequently overlooked is that of liberalizing or decontrolling exports. The control of exports is a basic feature of the traditional planned economy, and liberalization in this field by the removal of formal and informal controls is as important as the other institutional changes involved in the economic transition. To mention but one example, providing new small-scale exporters equal opportunity and the freedom to operate in this field is a precondition for the dynamic development of the private sector in Central and Eastern Europe.

In sum, trade liberalization (or foreign economic liberalization in general) is crucial to the establishment of a market economy. In Central and Eastern Europe there has been some debate over the timing of liberalization relative to privatization. Earlier, the idea that privatization should precede liberalization had some appeal. According to Tardos (1991, p. 256), "one can liberalize successfully only in those areas where the radical transformation of the ownership system has succeeded, and where privatization has already taken place." It is true that prerequisites for successful liberalization abound (Chapter 1), and there is some validity to the emphasis on the interrelations among the various elements of economic transition. In this sense, the sequencing of liberalization measures is dependent on the way in which structural and other changes in the economy occur. Practical experience suggests, however, that liberalization comes before privatization, whether governments opt for shock therapy or a gradual approach. Liberalization of foreign and domestic economic activity is a precondition for the development of a private sector.

Foreign Direct Investment and Economic Transition

Foreign direct investment is regarded as a powerful means for increasing macroeconomic efficiency, accelerating economic growth, and achieving integration into the international economy in many developing and newly industrializing countries. This assessment is often sufficient to explain the keen interest of the former socialist countries in Central and Eastern Europe in promoting such investment. Capital, technology, know-how, management skills, and new export markets are vital. There are, however, at least two additional factors that make foreign direct investment decisive in present-day Central and Eastern Europe. First, as indicated in the previous chapter, it is a means of systemic transformation where domestic savings are inadequate.[6] Second, because of the very significant external debt and problems of refinancing, it is a potentially important means of debt management.

Foreign direct investment means capital inflow that does *not* increase indebtedness—a crucial advantage for countries whose ability to service their debts remains to be demonstrated from day to day or that cannot service their debts at all. From the point of view of direct short-term balance-of-payments considerations, an increase in hard-currency inflows as a result of establishing foreign direct investment (as distinct from inflows in the form of productive or other assets) is the most welcome.[7] Of course, foreign direct investment cannot be regarded as a substitute for financial inflows; one reason this is so is that the restraint demanded by creditors can only have a negative effect on the behavior of investors.[8]

Despite a dynamic takeoff in the region (see below), direct investment inflow remains far below expectations. Those expectations were, however, illusory. There are numerous explanations for what Central and East Europeans perceive as a relative neglect of their region by multinational companies and other investors. Economic decline and structural deficiencies are as important as legitimate doubts regarding political stability. The small domestic markets of the Five do not always effectively attract investors with global strategies. In the wake of the end of CMEA, it is evident that these countries cannot be considered vehicles for penetration into the market of the former Soviet Union (it is even dubious whether investing in one of them would promote penetration into the markets of the others). Even after the completion of the association agreements of Poland, Czechoslovakia, and Hungary with the EC, it is not clear how their integration into the EC and the EFTA will progress (Inotai 1991). Those problems aside, investors' geographical priorities have also changed in recent years. Even if Central and Eastern Europe continues to be in fashion, for German investors the former GDR is paramount and for many others the Middle East (the postwar reconstruction of Kuwait) is a more attractive investment opportunity.

The close interrelationship between foreign direct investment and systemic transformation must not be underestimated. Needless to say, the outstanding role of such investment in privatization does not make the issues involved in transformation any easier to solve. For instance, the Hungarian government is seeking to increase foreigners' ownership share in the economy from the present 3.5–4 percent to 25 percent by 1994. Given myriad constraints, this target seems rather ambitious. Conversely, schemes of free distribution of state property in other countries are conceptually a rejection of any excessive dependence of privatization on foreign investment (although these countries do support a considerable influx of direct investment and a significant role for foreigners in the management of the economy).[9]

The principal disagreement on the subject of free distribution of state property has already been outlined. It is also clear, however, from international experience that extensive reliance on foreign direct investment is not a simple matter. In every country in the world, from the United States to India, coexistence with foreign investors is complicated. The typical political and economic arguments for and against foreign investment (especially those of national sovereignty and "selling out") have been raised in the Central and East European countries. *Hic et nunc,* the problem has some key elements which deserve elaboration.

First, the sovereignty argument has country-specific ramifications in Central and Eastern Europe. It may be a strong argument in Poland, where history clearly supports the belief that the country's independence may be endangered by the West, or in Czechoslovakia, especially in its economic relations with Germany. It is, however, a relatively weak argument in countries that have different experiences and no fears of potential conflict with foreign investors' home countries. As a rule, the sovereignty issue is not crucial in the present situation. The former CMEA economies were isolated from the international economy and characterized by a one-sided dependence on the Soviet Union for forty years. Integration with the West (here including direct investment by Western firms) is now perceived as a consequence of the discontinuation of the previous (dis)orientation. Thus, Central and East Europeans view regaining economic sovereignty and integration with the West as two parts of the same process. Of course, this point should not be overemphasized: the sovereignty argument certainly has some appeal in countries where national identity was restored most recently and nationalism is mounting. In fact, opposition to direct foreign investment is everywere related to opposition to modernization and opening up to the world. It is not by chance that the sovereignty argument has surfaced among populists of every stripe, traditionalists within the ruling parties, and advocates of the reestablishment of interwar patterns of social and political order. However, if economic deterioration persists and is attributed to a lack of anticipated Western assistance, present attitudes toward foreign direct investment may adjust accordingly.

The regulation of foreign direct investment has frequently been altered in recent years in Central and Eastern Europe. The most recent version is generally considered liberal by international standards. Hungary, for example, allows 100 percent foreign ownership without any licensing and places no limitations on the repatriation of profits and capital. Generous tax allowances and in some cases tax holidays are being offered to companies with foreign participation. In Poland, licensing is now required only in exceptional cases, profit repatriation is free, and tax allowances are offered in many instances. In Czechoslovakia, foreign owners can hold up to 100 percent of the capital and receive favorable tax incentives, and profit repatriation is free. There have been changes in a similar direction in Bulgarian and Romanian regulation as well.

The current, mostly liberal attitudes toward foreign direct investment in fact coexist with a tendency to limit foreigners' participation *in privatization* either institutionally (in Poland and Czechoslovakia) or in terms of proportion of total assets. Even in Hungary, the government employs a concept of *national* ownership in the process of privatization; certain state-owned industries or enterprises can be sold to domestic institutions or private individuals only.

Selling prices for state-owned enterprises are, as was mentioned in Chapter 2, not only difficult to establish but also the cause of domestic political warfare among the supporters of different privatization and foreign-investment strategies. However, it is in fact policies with regard to the pace of privatization that inspire protests against "selling-out" state property. It is obvious that one cannot sell a significant portion of the national wealth in a very short period of time at reasonable prices. An additional factor behind the low prices in Central and Eastern Europe is that foreign direct investment is in the initial stage of rapid development. However relatively rapid the process, the absolute number of potential Western investors willing to bid for large state-owned enterprises remains small.[10]

Perhaps more important are concerns other than prices. What is involved is whether expectations concerning the restructuring of state-owned enterprises as a result of selling them to foreign owners are fulfilled. Simply stated, an investor's strategic reasons for investing in an East European company[11] may eventually collide with the aims of short-term retooling, reorientation, and increase in hard-currency exports (usually the most important considerations on the East European side).

Governments that stress foreign direct investment in privatization must not overlook the fact that progress in privatization in different fields and sectors of the economy (what is to be sold and what is not) may effectively depend on where and how foreign investors are inclined to invest. However, if the idea of rapid privatization at all costs is abandoned, then the sectoral and regional priorities of foreign investors and emerging patterns of foreign investment will be important signals for adjustment in those sectors and fields of the economy where such investment is nonexistent or insignificant. More important, recent experience suggests that the most serious constraint on foreign direct investment in Central and Eastern Europe is not Western demand but domestic difficulties of varying types, ranging from unclear privatization strategies and legal and institutional conditions to red tape and deficiencies of infrastructure (notably communication) and relatively high rents for commercial space.

The critical point is that the involvement of foreign capital is *the only effective means for genuine privatization of state-owned enterprises in Central and Eastern Europe.* "Real" or "final" owners of enterprises are not guaranteed to emerge from this (in fact such owners often cannot be found, large Western investors being mostly public corporations), but this mode of privatization does persuade managers to act in accordance with efficiency criteria. "Western"-type management and marketing and company strategies adjusted to international market requirements in the former state-owned sector can be pursued in this way.

It can be argued that genuine privatization means the effective abandonment of government control over former state-owned enterprises, and this is where privatization through foreign direct investment seems much more straightforward than the various artificial schemes whereby governments or quasi-governmental bureaucracies retain an outstanding role in the management of enterprises for some time.

In addition, the development of a new, small-scale private sector—by definition not a domain for large multinational investors—is also largely supported by the inflow of Western investment. Most Western capital flows into joint ventures with large state-owned companies. Small-scale industries, services, and retail stores are much less capital-intensive, and Central and East European policy makers are not always very happy with the priority attached by the foreign investors to establishing joint ventures in those fields. In Hungary, for example, 47 percent of all joint ventures established in 1990 were in the trade sector, but that sector received only 19 percent of all invested foreign capital. Foreign investors have an impact on those sectors not so much through restructuring by way of large-scale investment into new technology as through improved management and marketing, clever strategies to close existing domestic market gaps, and so on. In some countries, it is because of small-scale Western investments that many sectors of the domestic (consumer) market have grown dynamically in recent years. This development may have had a greater effect on the functioning of the economy as a whole than the establishment of a relatively small number of large-scale joint ventures involving large multinationals.

However, some caution in evaluating the rapid increase in small-scale joint ventures without substantial investment on the part of the foreign partner is warranted. A number of *pseudo*-joint ventures have been established with the single aim of circumventing domestic taxes or foreign-exchange regulations. The liberal profit repatriation rules of joint ventures, for example, have fostered a specific Central and East European version of capital flight. Clearly, the idea of preferential treatment of joint ventures relative to domestic business is mistaken.

To conclude, for at least two reasons foreign direct investment cannot be regarded as a panacea for the economic dilemmas that the Five face. First, external and internal conditions do not allow for unrestricted direct investment inflow even in the countries that hope to rely the most on such investment for economic transition. Therefore it is not a recipe for rapid privatization. Second, apart from the sums that may be involved, international experience suggests that the benefits of foreign direct investment are inconclusive and the concept of using *foreign* investment as a means of *internal* systemic transition from a planned to a market economy is flawed. What is more, it is by no means evident that increase in such investment will automatically lead to improved macroeconomic performance and dynamic export growth in the short term. An additional problem is that under certain circumstances foreign direct investment may promote protectionism rather than competition. A recent example is Hungarian restrictions on automobile imports to ensure domestic markets for General Motors and Suzuki, whose Hungarian factories are about to start production (these investments have received large subsidies from the Hungarian government). In Poland, Fiat and General Motors have demanded higher tariffs on automobile imports as a condition for their purchase of Polish automobile factories. A related problem is that foreign direct investment may create new monopolies on the domestic market. A case in point is the sale of some domestic sectoral trading chains (for example, in shoes or cloth) to a single foreign buyer in Hungary.

Such difficulties and uncertainties notwithstanding, progress in the field of foreign investment will be crucial in the present stage of transition. Therefore, its necessary though insufficient role in *genuine* privatization and in the opening of the economy should not be underestimated. In the general framework outlined above, the prospects for foreign direct investment in Central and Eastern Europe will depend, to a large extent, on domestic economic and political developments, including privatization policies, and the development of foreign economic relations. As we have indicated, foreign credits can to a certain extent be substituted for investment. A dynamic long-term inflow of foreign direct investment will, however, clearly depend on increase in trade, balance-of-payments developments, institutional changes in economic relations with the West, and the whole complex of Western policy toward the countries of the region. These problems of international economic relations will be addressed in the following chapters. Before turning to an assessment of the problems and prospects of the Five's relations with the West, we have to address the issues of their traditional economic relations within the former CMEA. Successful policies of outward orientation will depend primarily on the strategic reorientation of trade relations from the former CMEA toward the West.

Notes

1. The first CMEA country to allow joint ventures was Romania, in 1971. Political as opposed to economic considerations were behind the decision, and no significant growth of foreign investment followed. In Hungary, joint ventures became possible in 1972, but no serious development in this field took place for a decade or so thereafter. Poland allowed foreign investors of Polish origin to invest in small-scale private industries in 1976. Bulgaria made legal provisions for joint venture activity in 1980 and Czechoslovakia in 1986.

2. For an assessment of the motives and strategies for and components of foreign economic liberalization in Central and Eastern Europe, see Köves and Marer (1991b). For a comprehensive overview of the issues of economic liberalization in former socialist economies from a global international perspective, see Köves and Marer (1991a).

3. Liberalization of imports figured high among the targets of the Hungarian economic reform of 1968. "Those enterprises which possess forints should be able to buy the corresponding amount of foreign exchange in order to import," it was proclaimed. However, except for the earliest period of reform and the end of 1980s, it was mostly the forms and mechanisms of controls rather than their content that changed (Gács 1991, p. 196).

4. Although a number of Hungarian policy makers seem to have entertained calls from outside to declare the Hungarian forint convertible at once.

5. For a more detailed account of Hungarian import liberalization policies, see Oblath (1991a) and Köves and Oblath (1991).

6. However, foreigners may invest in new enterprises as well, besides taking part in privatization by buying shares in state-owned firms.

7. Inflows of productive assets as a form of payment of the purchase price of equity (foreign direct investment in kind) mean imports of commodities that need not be paid for. Given the recession and balance-of-payments difficulties, the short-term importance of these inflows must also not be underestimated. In the long term, the inflow of productive assets is crucial for restructuring and export growth. Moreover, what is important is *net* hard currency inflows—effective inflows of hard currency as a result of foreign direct investment minus hard-currency outflows (i.e., repatriation of profits or capital) related to that investment. It is, however, reasonable to suppose (and it is also in accord with the most recent Hungarian experience) that in the initial years the dynamic inflow of foreign direct investment greatly exceeds the outflow. From a different perspective, it is important that while direct investment, *if profitable,* also involves hard-currency outflow from the importing country, interest on credit and bonds must be paid independent of the profitability of transactions involving credit financing (Köves and Oblath 1991).

8. This has been the experience of developing countries. In the wake of the debt crisis, the role of the developing world as a site for direct investment by the OECD countries has diminished. At the same time, the Asian newly industrialized countries with sound external financing positions have gained as investment sites at the expense of indebted Latin America (Langhammer 1991b, pp. 402–403).

9. In Czechoslovakia, "the objects of mass privatization are . . . exclusion of foreigners until better information exists, uncertainty is reduced, and there is a prospect of sales to foreigners at a fair price" (Begg 1991, p. 45).

10. According to data published by the United Nations, 88 percent of the 10,700 joint

ventures existing in the Five in December 1990 were established in the single year of 1990. Committed foreign capital represented $1,200 million in Hungary, $850 million in Czechoslovakia, $400 million in Poland, $129 million in Romania, and $74 million in Bulgaria. In sum, small-scale investment predominated. The average size of investment in Hungary did not exceed $240,000. It was even less in Poland but relatively large (more than $500,000) in Bulgaria and Czechoslovakia (OECD 1991a, p. 37). Preliminary data suggest additions to foreign capital of $1,400 million in Hungary, $700 million in Poland, $600 million in Czechoslovakia, and $140 million in Romania in 1991.

11. For example, preventing a Western competitor from purchasing the company, facilitating the restructuring of his *other* (home) companies by relocating traditional production to Central and Eastern Europe (more exactly, ensuring traditional supply from what the company in Central and Eastern Europe currently produces, and so on).

4

The End of the CMEA: Implications of the Change to Dollar-Accounted Trade

The first day of January 1991 will certainly prove to be a significant, perhaps turning, point in Central and Eastern Europe's modern economic history. It marked the change from transferable-ruble to dollar payments and world market prices in trade among the former CMEA countries. The change had the effect of destroying traditional trade flows and long-established chains of cooperation among the Five but also of offering new opportunities (see Chapter 5). The change to hard-currency trade with the former GDR, the number two country in intra-CMEA trade, was a consequence of the German Economic and Monetary Union and German reunification. Because of declining demand for East European manufactures and food in the former GDR, this change led to a sharp decline in the Five's exports. In many cases, the negative impact of the decline on their economies was exacerbated by the fact that valid commercial contracts worth hundreds of millions of roubles were annulled. The net effect of the GDR's joining the FRG will ultimately depend on developments in the Five's own trade with the reunited Germany. In all likelihood, however, this will be the most dynamic part of their foreign trade for years to come.

Approximately 60–70 percent of the *intra-CMEA trade* of the Central and East European countries was with the Soviet Union. Indeed, the greatest concern for the Five was how the change to dollar trade would affect their economic relations with the Soviets. Serious immediate consequences were foreseen, but the actual shock, in its severity, in certain respects defied all imagination.

Conventional wisdom dictated that because of the commodity composition of Soviet trade with its Central and East European partners and peculiarities of the intra-CMEA pricing system, the switch to dollar-accounted trade would mean a very significant (though of varying magnitude) terms-of-trade loss for *all* Central and East European countries. International oil-price hikes in the aftermath of the Iraqi invasion of Kuwait in the summer of 1990 gave the problem a truly dramatic character. According to some estimates (KOPINT-DATORG 1990), the combined energy import bill (i.e., the dollar cost of energy formerly imported from the Soviet Union and paid for in transferable rubles) of the Five for 1991 would reach $15 billion—a sum that these countries would find impossible to finance on their own. The message conveyed by these estimates was that without substantial Western financial assistance (a degree of financial support that Western banks and governments had been unwilling to offer before the shift to dollar trade) the already endangered economies of some or all of the Central and East European countries might well collapse. This would have unpredictable consequences for the whole process of systemic transformation as well as for the political stability of the region.

Actually, oil prices dropped as soon as the Gulf war broke out in early 1991, and the entire terms-of-trade problem was overshadowed by an almost total collapse of trade between the Five and the Soviets.[1] For all practical purposes, dollar-accounted trade amounted to very little in the first months of 1991. For the entire year, volumes of Central and East European exports to the former Soviet Union appear not to have exceeded 30–40 percent of the 1990 level. According to Soviet foreign trade statistics for the first nine months of the year (Table 4.1), while total Soviet exports in *value* terms (and expressed in domestic rubles) reached 70 percent and imports 56 per cent of the level of the same period of the previous year, Soviet exports to the Five amounted to 46, and imports from the Five to 38 percent of the level of the first nine months of 1990. Imports from Poland amounted to 30 percent, from Bulgaria and Hungary to 36–37 percent, and from Czechoslovakia to 43 percent of their level one year earlier.

The most immediate cause of the collapse was Soviet *inability* to pay for imports (in cases of change to *effective* hard-currency payments with such countries as Poland or Hungary) and Soviet *unwillingness* to export (notably when establishing some kind of bilateral clearing in hard currency). The immediate effect of the collapse of trade on the economies of the Five was a severe shock, as there were no ready alternative markets for the goods being produced for export to the Soviet Union. The collapse of exports was therefore the single most important reason for a new wave of difficulties: deepening recession, increasing unemployment, increased inflation, and more difficulties in balancing the budget.[2] To a large extent, it was because of this shock that a further deterioration of the economic situation in all of the Five during 1991 was unavoidable.

In this chapter various factors contributing to the trade crisis will be analyzed. It will be demonstrated that several real ("objective," in pretransformation East European parlance) economic difficulties are associated with the change from CMEA-type state trading to a largely market-based and dollar-accounted trade, in addition to mistakes and inadequacies in the preparatory work for and implementation of the shift. Nevertheless, the *single most important factor* behind the collapse in trade was the *Soviet economic and political crisis, eventually leading to a crash and disintegration.* In other words, a breakdown of commercial rela-

TABLE 4.1 The Collapse of Soviet Foreign Trade with the Five in 1991
(Soviet Foreign Trade, January–September 1990 and 1991)
(billion rubles at the commercial exchange rate)

	January–September 1990	January–September 1991	1991 Imports as Percentage of 1990 Level
Total			
Exports	86.8	60.6	69.8
Imports	101.4	57.0	56.2
Developed market economies			
Exports	38.4	34.2	89.1
Imports	48.2	32.1	66.6
Developing countries			
Exports	11.6	8.1	69.8
Imports	10.0	5.8	58.0
Former socialist countries			
Exports	36.7	18.3	49.9
Imports	43.1	19.1	44.3
The Five			
Exports	26.7	12.3	46.1
Imports	30.1	11.4	37.9
Bulgaria			
Exports	5.7	1.7	29.8
Imports	7.6	2.8	36.8
Czechoslovakia			
Exports	6.5	3.9	60.0
Imports	7.2	3.1	43.1
Hungary			
Exports	5.1	2.3	45.1
Imports	5.0	1.8	36.0
Poland			
Exports	5.8	3.1	53.4
Imports	9.0	2.7	30.0
Romania			
Exports	3.6	1.3	36.1
Imports	1.3	1.0	77.0

The data here are presented in domestic rubles converted at a "commercial" rate of R1.8 = $1 for the first nine months of 1991 and are not comparable to data in Table 4.2 and elsewhere expressed, according to the traditional Soviet statistical data system, in foreign-trade rubles.

Source: Russian (former Soviet) Central Statistical Committee, as reported by *Business Eastern Europe*, 10 February 1992.

tions was inevitable because of the developments in the Soviet Union even if the transferable-ruble system had survived through 1991. Therefore, suggestions for coping with the collapse of trade should be based on a realistic assessment of the political and economic collapse and the future prospects of the former Soviet Union.

The End of a Trading System

The end of the CMEA system is one of the most important aspects of systemic transformation for the countries concerned. The transition to dollar trade should be approached within the general framework of the abandonment of the CMEA in favor of market-type foreign economic relations. However great the short-term costs and risks of the transition, they do *not* imply that the system of intra-CMEA trade was of general benefit to Central and East European economic development. The smaller European CMEA countries did, in fact, enjoy more favorable terms of trade in their transferable-ruble trade with the Soviet Union than in their dollar-accounted trade with other countries. They were net exporters of relatively overpriced manufactures (as compared with the energy and raw materials of which they were importers). This meant that in any given period of time, Central and East Europeans had price benefits when exporting to and importing from the Soviet Union. This is what Marrese and Vanous (1983) have called "implicit subsidies." The price of those static advantages, however, proved to be very high. For instance, one of the major problems was that although the long-term stability of large-scale transactions used to be regarded as an important microeconomic benefit arising from intra-CMEA relations, in the course of the past few years it had become clear that this was mostly a politically motivated illusion and had even been responsible for mistaken strategic decisions on the macroeconomic, industry, and firm levels. The assumed advantages and stability of intra-CMEA trade for the Central and East European countries became a source of considerable uncertainty and weakness on the international markets and one of the main reasons for the external disequilibrium that has haunted them for more than a decade. As we put it as early as 1983:

> Development oriented to CMEA market required a different economic (sectoral and product) structure than increasing exports to the world market (and thus the latter as a development policy goal was neglected). It raised different requirements towards quality and the assortment of goods as well as towards marketing and—what is perhaps the most important—therefore, other economic mechanisms, relations between economic control agencies and enterprises, different enterprise and individual behavior, what is more, in many respects even other social policy priorities, science and educational policies were required and developed than those which could have served for successful activity on Western markets . . . (Köves 1983, pp. 128–129).

The traditional CMEA trade system was a tool for an inward-oriented, autarkic, and Soviet-dominated development strategy for member countries. It would be impossible to change to outward-oriented policies based on economic liberalization and reorientation of foreign economic relations without abolishing the CMEA type system and its structures of state trading: the coordination of plans and the annual intergovernmental trade agreements in which *governments* undertook commitments to supply and purchase commodities on terms established by quota (see Köves 1991).

As has been mentioned, it was in the last years of the CMEA system that the Hungarians suggested abolishing state trading in their relations with the Soviet Union and other CMEA countries. Their concern was not the operation of the CMEA (in fact they had become weary of twenty years of unsuccessful attempts at reforming it) but Hungary's role within the system. They wanted the logic of the economic system—that of an evolving market economy—prevailing on the Hungarian side, in which business decisions were made by firms while macroeconomic regulation was the task of government. Mechanisms incompatible with this aim, such as plan coordination, itemized government commitments for the purchase or supply of individual commodities, and limitations on enterprise independence and responsibility, were to be abolished. The focus of the Hungarian proposal was the transition to a new trade system, and the eventual change of the currency of trade (from the ruble to the dollar) was but a consequence of this systemic change.[3]

Changing the System or the Currency of Trade?

The actual change in January 1991 was based on another proposal originally made by the Soviets at the Sofia CMEA session in early 1990. The Soviet decision to change to dollar trade among CMEA countries was aimed primarily at changing the currency and the prices of trade; changing the trade system was simply a by-product of the transition to dollar-accounted trade. The Soviet proposal was a logical consequence of the political change taking place in Central and Eastern Europe. As may be clear from the above, the Soviet's calculation was that the shift to dollar trade and (world) market prices[4] would improve their terms of trade and result in either a larger volume of imports or increasing hard-currency earnings or both. From their perspective, it seemed senseless to grant preferential trade treatment to countries that no longer regarded themselves as political allies of the Soviet Union. As will be discussed later, these considerations contained at least one important element of miscalculation.

Dollar-accounted trade was not in itself incompatible with the CMEA-type system of state trading. In effect, the impediments to genuine business-based trade between the Five and the Soviet Union were very strong. Foreign trade was one of the few areas of the Soviet economy in which effective state (central) control survived. As for the Five, because of their competitive weakness on international markets, and the difficulties of reorientation of trade, their policy makers felt pressed to continue seeking Soviet state guarantees concerning both purchases of their exports and stable deliveries of Soviet raw materials. The bilateral intergovernmental agreements between the Central and East European countries and the Soviet Union concluded in late 1990 to regulate the change to dollar trade included indicative lists of goods that were to be traded in 1991. The original idea was that those lists could make the initial period of transition smoother but they were conceived as quotas of goods whose trade would be licensed by the respective governments (if export/import licenses were needed) when transactions between trading agents were concluded. However, the governments of the partner countries interpreted Soviet approval of the lists as a kind of *guarantee* of the allocation of the amount of foreign exchange needed for the realization of those transactions. Though this interpretation seemed logical given what they knew about the traditional Soviet foreign-trade system (though not about how it was actually operating in 1991), it was, as will be argued later, a misunderstanding. Nevertheless, a liquidity shortage in *all* of the former CMEA countries (not only in the Soviet Union) made the search for cash-saving ways to change to dollar-based trade inevitable. It was no accident that a kind of dollar clearing was set up for some bilateral relationships.

Notwithstanding these and other difficult problems, *systemic change* for intra-CMEA trade concurrent with the transition to accounting in dollars was unavoidable. To be sure, even before the de jure end of the Soviet Union it had become clear that a return to a CMEA-type system was impossible. The impediments to state trading were even greater than those to market-based trade. In principle, the transition to a market economy in the former CMEA countries rendered state trading in the long run inconceivable. The abolition of central planning, the foreign trade monopoly, and the subordination of economic agents to authorities, as well as effective liberalization and privatization of the economy in the reforming countries, destroyed the very foundations of the CMEA system. This is important even though the transition in the various domestic economies is proceeding at different rates and in some countries producing dubious outcomes.

More important from the point of view of short-term developments, state trading of the CMEA type was not based entirely on theoretical assumptions concerning the domestic economic systems of members. A further implicit assumption was that the governments were in control of their economies and would see that any obligation undertaken by them was fulfilled. However, this assumption was no longer valid in 1991, even for the Soviet Union, where the central bureaucracy controlled most foreign trade transactions but *not the economy*. Because of this lack of central control alone, governmental obligations for export deliveries (and import purchases) could no longer be honored. The economy of this huge country had become segmented by barter-type relations among republics, regions, and enterprises, and the domestic currency was being squeezed out by the dollar in many areas in which transactions occurred.

It is important to understand that the demise of the CMEA system was an outcome of the economic crisis of the member countries. The resultant overall decline in trade volumes that had begun earlier and became very considerable in 1990 *was unrelated to the imminent transition to dollar-accounted trade*. Effectively the Soviet Union, the central and strongest member of the CMEA, had lost its economic and political capability to hold the system together.

Transition Policies, 1989–1991

Confronted with Soviet determination to change to dollar accounting, the Central and East European countries had no choice but to accept the imminent transition. Cautiously declared intentions, notably by Czechoslovakia and Poland, to postpone it for several years (or to allow for a gradual phasing in of the new system) were abruptly dismissed. Clearly, positions among the Five differed markedly with the degree and character of their dependence on trade with the Soviet Union. Hungary was at one extreme, with the Soviet Union's share in total foreign trade falling below 20 percent by 1990, and trade reorientation toward the West already advancing. Bulgaria, at the other extreme, had almost totally Soviet-oriented development policies and trade. Despite these and other differences, all of the Five had to face dramatic short-term effects. Consequently each of them had been engaged in attempts at fashioning some kind of safety net to help finance the costs of the transition in its first and most difficult phase. It was argued that through continuous structural adjustment of national economies both their terms of trade and their trade balances would improve after the initial shock. The Five were also attempting to minimize the trade-reducing effects of the transition and to ensure smooth trading and financial arrangements for accomplishing it.

The Safety Net and the Problem of Transferable-Ruble Surpluses

The safety-net problem emerged in Hungary during the discussions over the Hungarian proposal to introduce systemic change in trade with the Soviets. It was apparent that if discontinuation of state trading was to involve a one-step changeover to hard-currency trade for Hungary, financial arrangements for covering the immense costs would be necessary (for an earlier statement of this problem, see Köves 1991). One approach was to set up a safety net within the framework of the Hungarian-Soviet relationship. The assumption was that the Soviets would be inclined to share the financial burden of the transition. Another approach was to build the safety net within the framework of Western assistance to the transformation process in Central and Eastern Europe. Given the abolition of state trading as one of the fundamental conditions for transition to a market economy, this was undoubtedly a reasonable approach, and it will be discussed in later chapters. Suffice it to say here that no large-scale Western assistance for the transition to dollar-based trade was in fact received. The unusually large financial burden attributable to the transition was, however, addressed in agreements between the respective Central and East European governments and the IMF in shaping balance-of-payments and other financial targets for 1991.

With the benefit of hindsight, a Soviet-financed version of the safety net seems romantic and impractical. It is evident that in 1990 or 1991 the Soviets had neither the political reason nor the economic capability to offer financial assistance to the Five, especially to Hungary, Czechoslovakia, or Poland. They were right in believing that, whatever the financial burden of the transition for the Five, the Soviet Union was really much more in need of financial help. As obvious as this statement is, the safety-net idea did not sound as nonsensical at the outset as it does today. The Soviet economic situation was somewhat less critical than it later became, and political relations between the Soviets and their CMEA partners were sounder. Accordingly, the idea that, because of the long-term interests and advantages for both countries inherent in the transition to a new system of relations, short-term burden sharing would be justifiable and effective enjoyed some popularity and support in the Soviet Union. A joint document in September 1989 concerning the transition to dollar-accounted trade between Hungary and the Soviet Union and presented to their respective governments by the joint Hungarian-Soviet Committee of Economists (a body set up by the respective Academies of Science) stressed this point.[5] Later, at the Sofia session of the CMEA, Czechoslovakia and Poland also asked to share the costs of the transition, and apparently it was agreed at that meeting that the shift to hard-currency settlements should be implemented through policy measures ("shock absorbers") that would help to prevent one-sided losses and benefits (ECE 1991).

Despite all this, the safety-net idea in its pure form was never seriously discussed on the governmental level. It was raised, however, in a specific economic context and proved to have effects very different from those originally intended. In 1989, Hungary accumulated a large surplus in its current transferable-ruble account with the Soviet Union (about TR800 million).[6] Because the CMEA system had not produced any practicable solutions for making use of trade balances but the fate of the surplus was important because of the imminent transition to dollar settlements, a Hungarian-Soviet understanding was reached in the spring of 1990 concerning recalculation of this surplus in dollars at the rate of TR1 = $0.92. The understanding was that the surplus of $700 million or so would be credited to Hungary's account with the change to dollar trade scheduled for 1991. (The parties agreed that the eventual further ruble balances would be recalculated in dollars at the same rate.) The informal but widely published understanding was that this sum would be used for financing the anticipated Hungarian hard-currency deficit in trade with the Soviet Union *during 1991*. Although credit could not have been extended for financing Hungarian trade deficits with countries other than the Soviet Union, even in the case of deficits arising from the change to dollar trade with the Soviets (e.g., oil imports for dollars from sources other than the Soviet Union), the Hungarian government hoped that this understanding would solve at least the majority of the short-term financial problems related to the transition to dollar accounting.

The TR1 = $0.92 rate compared unfavorably, from the Soviet point of view, with the official transferable-ruble-to-dollar cross-rate of the Hungarian National Bank (about TR1 = $0.45 in 1990). Still the Soviets were satisfied with the agreed upon terms. Their real objective at the time was to maintain the flow of imports from Hungary even if Soviet deliveries further declined. Although a significant cutback of Hungarian exports in 1990 could not be avoided, subsequent Hungarian governments were unable to resist pressure from exporters to disregard trade balancing requirements, and this resulted in a further significant surplus on the Hungarian transferable-ruble account.[7]

In Hungary, the rude awakening came in June 1990, when the Soviets withdrew their promise to settle the debt in 1991 and instead insisted on a five-year repayment period. The net result for Hungary was a $1.7-billion resource outflow without any certainty as to the time and terms of its repayment instead of a safety net for financing the expected 1991 deficit.

A similar agreement covering the recalculation of transferable-ruble balances in dollars was concluded between the Soviet Union and Czechoslovakia. The rate (TR1 = $1) was even more favorable for Czechoslovakia than that decided upon with the Hungarians, but the debt repayment was scheduled to begin only after 1995. Czechoslovakia accumulated a surplus of about TR3.8 billion vis-à-vis the Soviet Union in 1989–90 (*Hospodárské Noviny,* 11 April 1991). The Polish surplus for the period between January 1990 and February 1991 reached about TR7.7 billion, whereas smaller surpluses were accumulated by Romania (TR400 million) and Bulgaria (TR500 million) (Richter 1991). In the wake of Soviet disunion there is no reliable information concerning the fate of these surpluses, but it may well be that it makes no difference whether any agreement was made.[8]

Negotiating Transition

The other ambition of the Five was to minimize or at least to monitor the trade-reducing effects of the transition to dollar-accounted trade. Unfortunately, this policy proved no more successful than the efforts at creating a safety net.

The governments tried hard to check the contraction of both imports from and exports to the Soviet Union. For example, even though starting in 1991 Soviet (Russian) oil was traded against dollars at international market prices, they still wanted to ensure as many Soviet oil deliveries to themselves as possible. In fact, imports of oil from the former Soviet Union seem to have some competitive advantages over oil from sources. For instance, Czechoslovakia lacks the necessary infrastructure (pipelines) for importing significant quantities of oil from other countries. (A new pipeline to its refineries from Ingolstadt [Germany] that could make it independent of Russian oil imports when completed in 1994 or 1995 is in the planning stage.) Apart from that, the lower transportation costs involved in importing Soviet oil, knowledge of the Soviet oil trade, and lack of experience in international oil trade may help explain this pattern of behavior. Of greater significance, and in the spirit of their traditional approach to trade with the Soviet Union, the Five regarded Soviet oil and other energy imports as a key to maintaining their (manufacturing) exports to the Soviet Union.[9]

It is worth mentioning that the reasoning behind CMEA traditions and state

TABLE 4.2   Oil Imports from the Soviet Union by the Five, 1988–1991 (million metric tons)

	1988	1989	1990	1991 (First Half)	1991 (Total Import Demand[a])
Bulgaria	12.7	12.6	7.8	1.8	11.0
Czechoslovakia	16.8	16.9	13.0	5.0	13.0
Hungary	8.4	7.8	4.8	1.4	6.5
Poland	15.8	15.2	9.7	3.9	13.0
Romania	4.0	3.9	3.4	0.1	16.0

[a] Estimates.

Source: Based on data in Sándor Richter, "Is There a Future for Regional Economic Cooperation in Eastern Europe?" (paper presented at the conference "Whither Socialist Society" held in Jerusalem, Israel, 8–13 April 1991) and, for first half of 1991, in *PlanEcon Energy Report*, no. 3, December 1991.

trading rests on the preoccupation of the importing governments with stability rather than with concrete economic considerations. They wanted to settle the issue with the Soviets prior to and quite independently of any negotiations regarding imports from other sources. Symptomatic of this approach was the tendency of the press in the Five to consider the amounts of oil *promised* by the Soviets (often in a non-binding way) independent of any strings attached, as a kind of "success indicator" of the respective governments with regard to economic relations with the Soviet Union. This approach is not only (theoretically) counterproductive but also, as the experience of the recent past suggests, a source of considerable instability and additional costs if oil deliveries should fall short of expectations (plans) and therefore require emergency imports (expensive by definition) from other sources.

Central and East European oil imports from the Soviet Union further decreased in 1991 (Table 4.2). Total 1991 imports may have been roughly half (in some cases well below that) of both 1988 levels of imports from the Soviet Union and the estimated total present import demand. This is an inevitable consequence of declining Soviet oil production, declining total oil exports, and the reorientation of Soviet exports from the former CMEA countries to the West. All the available evidence (and not only the worst-case scenario according to which the former Soviet Union will become a net oil importer) suggests that the continuing sharp decline of oil production in the former Soviet Union will lead to an even sharper drop in its exports to the Five in 1992.

As has been indicated, dilemmas concerning their export policies in relation to declining imports from the Soviet Union have afflicted Central and East European policy makers for some time. The transition to dollar-based trade added a new dimension to the problem. It was evident that the attitudes of Soviet importers toward East European goods would change if they had to pay for them in dollars. They might opt for buying Western goods instead or for importing from the Five at discounted prices. There was no indication whatsoever how large those discounts might be, and there was total uncertainty concerning how frequently and under what circumstances the Soviets would opt for the former or for the latter.

It is important to underline that the collapse that came to pass was *not* due to these structural problems associated with the exports of the Five. The positions of Central and East European exporters on the Soviet market prior to the transition to dollar-accounted trade were sometimes underestimated. As a matter of fact, a variety of factors strengthened those positions. Considering the traditional Soviet orientation of their economic and trade development, the reasons are apparent. Central and East European commodities may have been below world market standards, but a large proportion of them certainly generated a favorable image in the Soviet Union. By all accounts they were of much higher quality than the comparable domestic products. In many cases, Central and East European commodities were the only ones available. It was not only that Central and East Europeans had a relatively good knowledge of the Soviet market and its traditions and practices and of the Russian language but also that their products and producers were the ones Soviet importers and end users knew. In many fields of manufacturing, the great advantage of Central and East European firms was the repair and service network they had established all over the Soviet Union. Spare parts for the transport, chemical, agricultural, and other equipment of Central and East European origin used throughout the Soviet Union were badly needed. In those fields, there was little chance of substituting Western products for Central and East European imports. It follows that, for a number of economic, technological, and human reasons, not only did the Five depend to a large extent on the Soviet Union but the Soviet Union depended on the Five. Therefore, although a certain degree of trade contraction was considered inevitable, there was nothing inherent in the transition to dollar payments to suggest an eventual *collapse* of exports.

As has been pointed out, the Five had different ideas about how to control the decline of their exports to the Soviet Union. Some countries insisted on establishing hard-currency clearing with the Soviet central government in the hope that this would be the most efficient way of checking the decline. They sought to include as many of their exportables as possible in the clearing agreements in an effort to get effective Soviet government guarantees against any impediments to their exports. Other countries offered a somewhat similar explanation for the attachment of indicative lists to nonclearing-type trade agreements (although typically such lists covered less than 30–40 percent of the trade of the previous year). Agreements between the Five and the governments of various Soviet republics were put on the agenda as well, and these too were to include indicative lists. (The Soviet central government refused to include food on the indicative lists for imports, insisting that it be imported by the republics at their own cost.) Barter-type agreements with Soviet regions, cities, and firms were also suggested.

It is no exaggeration to say that nothing worked. The lack of preparation of the commercial and financial authorities (concerning, for example, banking procedures or guarantees related to the transition to dollar-accounted trade) and of trading agents on every side contributed to this general failure. It is worth mentioning that the way in which the new trade regime was expected to function was concealed from the public (including exporters and importers) until after the transition.

As has been indicated above, the actual collapse can be explained only in the light of Soviet economic and political developments. The Five clearly attempted to come to some agreement with the Soviet central government that would define the trading framework after the transition to dollar-accounted trade, but the Soviet government in 1991 lacked the authority to guarantee that agreements would be respected. Clearing agreements did not work because Soviet exporters confronted with domestic inflation and the impossibility of buying commodities on domestic markets *for rubles* were not inclined to accept anything short of "real" hard currency, that is, cash payment. This was an obstacle for Central and East European exports as well without a return to accumulating unusable surpluses on the clearing account. Nonclearing-type arrangements with the central authorities did not work because of the Soviet's inability to pay for imports. Hungarian and Polish firms exporting the commodities on the indicative lists signed by their respective governments and the Soviets rushed to enter into contracts with their Soviet counterparts and produced the commodities to be exported. The Soviets, however, failed to open the necessary letters of credit, and therefore export deliveries could not take place. Late in the summer of 1991, Hungarian deliveries against letters of credit opened by the Soviets did not exceed $165 million, as compared with about $1.5 billion anticipated for the year by the indicative lists. For the whole year, letters of credit valued at less than $400 million were opened. (*Napi Világgazdaság,* 21 January 1992). The press has widely publicized reports and interviews concerning the letter-of-credit problem. At the outset, the policy makers of the Five made every effort to explain the situation in terms of technical difficulties related to the transition. Their opponents, in turn, attributed the problem to mistaken (unfriendly) government policies toward the Soviet Union. Soon it became quite clear that the Soviet inability to pay was a general problem in its relations not only with the former CMEA but also with the Western countries.[10] This phenomenon was to be attributed to the increasing difficulty of servicing the country's hard-currency debt.[11] The idea of developing trade with the Soviet republics collided with the lack of real republican authority and autonomy concerning foreign economic relations (including an absence of republican banks authorized to deal with foreign exchange transactions) and the general confusion concerning the division of rights and responsibilities between federal and republican authorities. Barter trade was prohibited by the Soviet government in late 1990 for fear of hard-currency losses to the central budget.[12] A severe export tax (amounting to 5–50 percent of the selling price) also aimed at centralizing hard-currency earnings. Although some doors had been left open for firm-to-firm relations, the chances for developing decentralized trade with the Soviets were clearly very slim.[13]

Policy Options for the Five

The quagmire of 1991 was similar to what the Five had been dealing with for some years but the dramatic elements of the new situation made their choice more difficult and significant. These elements included the Soviet collapse and subsequent disintegration, the exceptionally serious breakdown of the Five's trade with the former Soviet Union, and the deepening economic crisis in Central and Eastern Europe. Therefore, discussions concerning trade strategies toward their large Eastern neighbor(s) were reopened in the aftermath of the change to dollar-accounted trade in 1991.

Answers concerning what strategy to adopt depended on whether one attributed the collapse to short-term factors or long-term ones. The key word for the former was *survival*. A relatively strong school of thought, supported by vested interests, contended that the difficulties in economic relations, at least in their dramatic version of early 1991, were due to nonrecurring or short-term factors, such as the deterioration of political relations, the technical difficulties of the transition to dollar-based trade, and Soviet balance-of-payments problems. Representatives of this school suggested that the worst for the Five might soon be over—that Soviet solvency might be restored as a result of the improving international political climate and Western assistance[14] and that the central authorities might regain control over economic processes (and/or decline to obstruct decentralized trade), allowing for government-level agreements with the Soviet Union and the reestablishment of the stability in trade relations that would allow Central and East European export growth. As strange as it seems, this kind of reasoning, sometimes in less explicit form, has effectively survived the dismemberment of the Soviet Union. What is stressed by its partisans is that even with the Soviet Union gone and its successors in economic and political disarray, there is still ample opportunity for trade with former Soviet territories (where there is a tremendous demand for foreign goods as well as commodity funds to be offered in exchange), especially for finding local partners in different republics.

The most popular theory of this school in Central and Eastern Europe and outside it is that withdrawal from the former Soviet market would amount to suicide. Clearly, survival means continued exports, even if the Russians and others do not or cannot settle their bills, but one must bear in mind that even a short-term policy of unilateral exports on the part of the Five would mean offering large-scale new credits to the successor states of the Soviet Union that could be financed by an inflating domestic currency and/or by the West. Even the miserable 1991 export performance of the Five in the Soviet market was in part due to credits or export credit guarantees offered by their governments. Given their already destabilized economy and heavy debt burden and the West's inability and/or unwillingness to increase its engagement in Central and Eastern Europe (see Chapter 7), the idea of offering large-scale new credits to the Soviet Union seems unjustifiable. The much publicized idea of maintaining Central and East European exports of food, medicines, and so on, by obtaining partial Western financing of those deliveries (a joint Polish, Hungarian, and Czechoslovakian proposal presented most vigorously at the Washington conference on humanitarian aid to the post-Soviet republics in January 1992) may be admirable but not very promising. In fact, Western governments and the EC are interested above all in financing exports of their own produce in the framework of humanitarian aid, especially in the face of the tremendous accumulated food stocks in Europe and elsewhere. Therefore, the Five should divest themselves of the illusion that participation in the international humanitarian aid program is a key to the stabilization of their trade with the former Soviet Union.

It is sometimes argued that a retreat from the former Soviet market would be unreasonable given the large size and potential of that market, which not long ago was very attractive to the West. Of course, what we are discussing is *not* a voluntary exit but an economic necessity, and there is no general rush for the markets of the former Soviet territories even though many Western companies are cautiously establishing themselves in the former Soviet Union. Apart from this, however, there is an immense difference between *entering* a market—establishing some sort of operation there in the framework of a network of global operations—and having a one-sided dependence on sales to or purchases from this market. The former is currently the case for most of the Western companies in the former Soviet Union, whereas the latter is the typical situation for the Central and East Europeans. This explains why Western strategies in the post-Soviet republics cannot be a compass for the Five.

It is important to note, for argument's sake, that considering the terrible Soviet economic decline of 1991 (as distinct from the other considerations mentioned above), the Soviet insistence on a one-step change to dollar-accounted trade in 1991 (instead of the more gradual approach advocated by Poland and Czechoslovakia) and the way in which the change was carried out by the Soviet authorities were also awkward and largely counterproductive. They actually led to *fewer* Soviet imports in 1991. Expectations concerning further international oil-price rises proved unfounded. More important, if the domestic economy and hard-currency trade had been functioning more or less normally, the transition would have substantially improved the Soviets' terms of trade and balance of payments. In the highly unusual Soviet circumstances of 1991, the most significant effect of the switch for the Soviet Union was the virtual *halt in the Five's exports*. Contrary to expectations, the Soviets cut their imports from the Five not because they had found other sources of imports on more favorable terms but simply because they had no choice. Total Soviet imports (from all sources) declined by 44 percent in the first nine months of 1991 as compared with the same period in

The End of the CMEA 73

TABLE 4.3 Soviet Foreign Trade, 1980–1990 (billion foreign trade, or transferable rubles at current prices)

	1980	1983	1984	1985	1986	1987	1988	1989	1990
Total									
Exports	46.9	67.9	74.4	71.7	68.3	68.1	67.1	68.3	60.9
Imports	44.5	59.6	65.3	69.4	62.6	60.7	65.0	71.1	70.7
Balance	5.1	8.3	9.1	2.2	5.7	7.4	2.1	−3.8	−9.8
CMEA									
Exports	24.3	34.4	38.2	40.2	42.2	40.7	39.0	37.8	26.2[a]
Imports	21.4	30.8	34.6	37.9	37.8	38.9	39.8	40.6	31.4[a]
Balance	2.9	3.6	3.6	2.3	4.4	1.8	−0.8	−2.8	−4.8[a]
Developed market economies									
Exports	15.9	19.7	21.4	18.6	13.1	14.2	14.7	16.4	22.0[b]
Imports	15.7	18.7	19.6	19.3	15.9	13.9	16.3	20.5	28.1[b]
Balance	0.2	1.0	1.8	−0.7	−2.8	0.3	−1.6	−4.1	−6.1[b]
Developing countries									
Exports	6.9	10.5	10.9	9.6	9.6	9.8	9.6	9.8	8.5
Imports	5.1	7.2	7.5	7.6	4.9	4.7	5.3	7.0	6.7
Balance	1.8	3.3	3.4	2.0	4.7	5.1	4.3	2.8	2.2

[a] The former GDR excluded.
[b] The former GDR included.

Source: Vneshnaya Torgovlia SSSR, Statistical Yearbook, Annual Series; for 1990, *Ekonomika i Zhizn*, no. 18 (April 1991).

the previous year (Table 4.1). Imports from developed market economies dropped by 33 percent and those from the Five by above 62 percent. Thus the collapse shocked not only Central and East European exporters. Specifically, it had the most unfavorable effects on many branches of the Soviet economy that depended on Central and East European deliveries by deepening the chaos and increasing the shortages in particular fields. For example, the Soviet Union succeeded in maintaining import levels (in value terms, to be sure) from the CMEA countries up until 1990 in spite of the great decline in its exports, and the net result was a Soviet deficit valued at 4.8 billion transferable rubles in the last year of the CMEA's existence (Table 4.3). (This sum disregards trade with the former GDR; with the GDR included, the deficit was nearly TR10 billion.) Given the peculiar CMEA-type clearing, it can be said that the Soviet Union succeeded in importing very significant amounts of Central and East European goods that were badly needed in the country without the necessity of fully balancing them with Soviet deliveries or hard currency payments. These same goods are scarce in the former Soviet Union today.[15]

Even prior to the August 1991 coup and the dissolution of the Union, traditional central planning had lost its relevance in the country. The functioning of the Soviet "nonsystem," as the Hungarian economist László Csaba (1991) has called it, presented serious impediments to doing business with the Soviets. In the last years of the existence of the Soviet state, almost complete uncertainty concerning the future of the economic system and the prospects of economic stabilization had rendered long-term thinking about economic relations nearly impossible. This uncertainty was well illustrated in the many reform schemes that were prepared and published in rapid succession during the last years and became obsolete in a matter of months or weeks as the economic and political situation changed.

Naturally, all of the difficulties of economic transformation in postcommunist countries discussed in previous chapters pertain to the former Soviet Union as well. Adding the seventy-year history of socialism in this country (instead of the forty years or so in Central and Eastern Europe) to the psychological and behavioral consequences of militantly antimarket education and ideology, economic backwardness, and the current cruel crisis, the reasons for the uncertainty or unpredictability of economic developments are evident. Post-Soviet economic prospects are obscured, however, in the first instance by the political instability resulting from the country's disintegration and fragmentation. The tremendous hazards of the economic and political collapse were accentuated by the coup. In the subsequent months it became certain that the failure of the Stalinist comeback had simply eliminated one possible source of danger. What is being called the "end of communism" in the Soviet Union did not signify a turning point in the process of disruption and disintegration. Quite the contrary, political and economic chaos and disintegration were to continue and deepen. The overriding danger concerning the newly created Commonwealth of Independent States is that political struggles among and within the republics (members of the Commonwealth or nonmembers) and the underlying, perhaps long-term uncertainty will preclude the emergence of meaningful economic policies for years to come. This means that considerations mentioned above in connection with policy options for the Central and East European countries remain valid in the aftermath of the Soviet dissolution.

What follows for the Five is the inadmissibility and impracticability of policies based on a strategy of survival on the former Soviet market. The experience of 1991 suggests that there is no way for them to survive the Soviet economic collapse by maintaining their exports to Russia and the other new republics. As distinct from this, many Central and East European firms have fairly strong positions on the post-Soviet market, and their continuing presence, aggressive marketing efforts extending to every possible partner, and good luck will help them to export and be paid for it. In spite of all the constraints, the governments of these countries can have some influence over the painful transition to the new trading system by creating the political and technical framework for it. At the same time, they must make it absolutely clear to firms engaged in post-Soviet trade that exports will not be subsidized and that they will not undertake any obligations on their behalf as to the risks and costs of exports or bail them out if they cannot collect their claims.

The short-term costs of this policy will undoubtedly be high; government intervention to support the sectors or firms in greatest need and thus prevent a general crash may be unavoidable. But there is no way of reducing these costs; there is no solution to the problems of trade with the former Soviet Union *within* its own framework. The only solution, however difficult, is trade reorientation. What the governments have to offer firms, in the first instance, is various forms of *assistance in reorientation*, the restructuring of production, and the identification of new prospective markets, including incentives for foreign investment in the fields concerned and some help in funding reorientation costs (presumably by preferential credits).

What the above narrative suggests, however, is that 1991 has proved to be a year of strategic change in the Five's foreign economic relations. The former Soviet Union has ceased to be the focus of their strategic trade orientation. What Central and East European policies can and must focus on is halting the decline (as soon as the situations of their partners permit) and stabilizing bilateral trade with the post-Soviet republics while eliminating the economic dependencies of past decades. Given the sorry state of affairs in the successor states of the Soviet Union, even that will not be an easy task.

Notes

1. This is not to say that terms-of-trade losses for the Five with the Soviet Union were not heavy. For instance, according to *PlanEcon Report's* preliminary estimates (9 December 1991), Soviet terms-of-trade vis-à-vis the former "ruble area" (a notion somewhat broader than the Five) improved by about 23 percent in 1991.

2. In some countries, such as Hungary, transferable-ruble trade was a source of significant budgetary income. This was mainly a consequence of taxing away a large part of the difference between domestic prices of imported energy and raw materials, which were based on world market prices, and the lower import prices.

3. Some versions of the Hungarian proposal did not call for any currency change. For example, one suggestion was to retain a kind of ruble clearing according to all the old rules (coordination of plans and commodity quotas) except the obligatory agreements concerning the supply and the purchase of individual commodities. All quotas were to be regarded as indicative. In this way, as far as Hungary was concerned, only the firms would take on supply or purchasing commitments after all the conditions of the agreement had been cleared (Oblath 1990).

4. Instead of the notorious intra-CMEA pricing system called the Bucharest price principle, according to which prices in any given year were calculated, at least theoretically, as average world prices over the previous five-year period.

5. The unpublished document, entitled "Joint Opinion of Soviet and Hungarian Experts concerning the Restructuring of the Trade System between the U.S.S.R. and Hungary," was signed by academician Oleg Bogomolov, director of the Moscow Institute of Economics of the World Socialist System (later renamed the Institute for International Economic and Political Research), and János Deák, the head of KOPINT-DATORG (the Institute for Economic and Market Research and Informatics). According to this docu-

ment, "considering the exceptionally great socio-political significance of the transition to the new system for both countries, state organs have to do their utmost to exclude the emergence of one-sided losses or gains for one or other party during the process of this transition." To avoid one-sided Hungarian losses, the document suggested the use of different sources of financing for bilateral trade: conversion of the Hungarian transferable-ruble surplus into dollars, extension of price preferences to Hungarian exporters to encourage additional production of commodities of special interest to the Soviet economy, Soviet investment in Hungarian firms whose production was being exported to the Soviet Union, and medium-term and long-term Soviet credits to Hungary on preferential terms.

6. Here and in the following, transferable ruble (TR) as the regular "currency" of transactions and unit of account in intra-CMEA trade should be distinguished from Soviet foreign trade ruble, a statistical concept for expressing Soviet trade data with any country (or all countries) also including trade transacted in hard currencies. Officially declared dollar values of the TR and the Soviet foreign trade ruble were close but not necessarily identical. Both the TR and the Soviet foreign trade ruble have to be distinguished from the domestically used money in the Soviet Union, the ruble.

7. What is more, Hungarian and Polish deliveries (and those of other countries) to the Soviet Union on the transferable-ruble account continued *after* the change to dollar trade, until the end of March. The agreements concerning the transition to dollar trade had left the door open for this. Exporters received the return from sales according to the old rules of the transferable-ruble trade (i.e., from their respective central banks) even if the Soviets were unable to settle their accounts. This largesse resulted in an additional surplus in both countries, in Poland reaching the incredible sum of TR2.2 billion by February 1991. In the case of Czechoslovakia, transferable-ruble exports to the Soviet Union between January and March 1991 reached TR390 million (Research Institute for Foreign Economic Relations 1991, p. 51.).

8. There are many other unsettled financial issues between the Five and the Soviet Union related to the transition. One is the old Polish debt to the Soviet Union, amounting to about TR4.3–4.7 billion (in addition, Poland owes the Soviet Union $1.7 billion), and another has to do with CMEA joint investment projects in the Soviet Union, notably the largest of these, the multibillion-dollar Yamburg-Tengiz complex. Problems concerning the liquidation of the two CMEA banks in Moscow (the International Bank for Economic Cooperation and the International Investment Bank) and the CMEA itself are also unresolved. Unrelated to the transition are mutual financial claims connected with the withdrawal of Soviet troops from Central and Eastern Europe (Soviet claims were mostly for property transferred to countries from which they withdrew, and Central and East European claims were for ecological damage caused by Soviet military bases in their countries) (Csaba 1991a, Richter 1991, Szabó-Szuba 1991).

9. As a matter of fact, the Soviets have insisted on handling the majority of their crude-oil exports to the Five separately, *outside* the indicative lists, to avoid any linkage between oil deliveries and imports of any kind from Central and Eastern Europe. They have regarded this as a way of ensuring a much-needed net hard-currency surplus in trade with the former CMEA countries. This idea may work as long as they have the necessary amount of oil to deliver and their partners the hard currency to pay for it. Nevertheless, according to the typical thinking in the Five, if the Soviets are guaranteed a hard-currency surplus in this way they may be persuaded to obligate themselves to import Central and East European commodities with a value amounting to, say, 60–70 percent of their exports. This thinking has proved wrong.

10. In Finland, change from clearing to hard-currency trade with the Soviet Union also took place in 1991, and Finnish estimates predicted a 50 percent decline in trade for the year (ETLA 1991). Actually, according to Soviet statistics for nine months of 1991, Soviet exports to Finland were 67 percent and imports from Finland 24 percent of the level of the corresponding period of the previous year. Soviet imports from Austria declined by 29 percent, from the United Kingdom by 56 percent, and from Sweden by 45 percent.

11. Obviously, there was no overall cessation of imports to the Soviet Union, and if some hard currency imports were being financed and others not it was a matter of preferences. It is an open question whether there is any likely explanation for these preferences (mainly for imports from the West) other than strictly economic ones concerning the commodity patterns of these imports—Soviet attraction to high-technology imports and essential food (imported at preferential prices from the West). The Soviets, however, were not inclined to use even hard-currency earnings from exports to Poland and Hungary to purchase imports from those countries. This policy can in part be explained in terms of the Soviet hard-currency shortage, but it can also be interpreted as a sign of a conscious neglect. This latter point was emphasized time and again in 1991 by Soviet experts on trade with Central and Eastern Europe as well. Behind this policy may have been the Soviet conviction that they need not pay because the governments of those countries would be unable to resist domestic pressures to maintain exports to the Soviet Union even if they did not. This has yet to be demonstrated.

12. This prohibition was formally lifted by the Pavlov government in the summer of 1991 but only for Soviet machinery and manufacturers, when what those countries in fact wanted to import from the Soviet Union was mostly raw materials. Many other restrictions have also remained.

13. In principle, exports of commodities that did not figure on any indicative list or in barter agreements were also not excluded. In that case, the Soviet importing firm had to have available the necessary amount of foreign exchange collected on the basis of its retention quota, which was generally relatively small and differentiated.

14. For example, prior to Gorbachev's visit to Japan in April 1991, the expectation in Central and Eastern Europe was that the problem of Soviet hard currency arrears (estimated at the time to have reached $7 billion) could be solved by returning or "selling" the disputed islands (annexed in 1945 by the Soviet Union) to Japan.

15. This is not to say that survival of the CMEA system into 1991 would have meant the maintenance of the 1990 level of Soviet imports from the Five, including nearly R5 billion in imports on (to say the least) very soft credit terms. Although experience (including the recent experience of 1991) suggests that the governments of the Five are much weaker in resisting pressures against unpaid exports when trade is accounted in transferable rubles, they would have been incapable of maintaining their 1989 and 1990 export policies in the face of obviously further declining Soviet deliveries. Trade collapse was inevitable in any case, but pressing on it was certainly a mistake on the Soviet's part due to misjudgments concerning their domestic economy and hard-currency situation.

5

Economic Integration and Cooperation in Postcommunist Central and Eastern Europe

When the "Soviet bloc" disintegrated and its former members declared their intention to "join Europe," the closed intraregional cooperation system directed at maintaining and developing the bloc's economic base and tying Central and Eastern Europe to the Soviet economy, thus creating a one-sided dependence on the Soviet Union, also became irrelevant. The developments that led to a joint decision to abandon the CMEA occurred as quickly as the process of political change. The crucial Sofia CMEA session in January 1990 in which the change to dollar-accounted trade was decided took it for granted that the switch-over to the new trade system would be implemented *within* the CMEA framework. Participants in the session suggested "a decisive renewal of the whole system of mutual co-operation within the CMEA framework, the fundamental renewal of the activities of the council, a verification of its functions and aims, and the preparation of a new statute" (*Pravda*, 11 January 1990; *Financial Times*, 11 January 1990) and not the abolition of the organization. It was in connection with the Sofia session that the Czechoslovak finance minister Vaclav Klaus raised the question of his country's eventual withdrawal from the CMEA, but his government felt it necessary immediately to denounce such an idea.

The times, however, had changed, and in June of the same year the committee that had been established in Sofia to discuss different views on the *reconstruction* of the CMEA recommended its transformation into a new organization. On the basis of a relatively broad consensus of member countries, the committee suggested setting up a loose organization of intraregional cooperation with (formal) functions very similar to those of the OECD. The idea was that the new organization would be responsible for analysis of the economic development of member countries and for cooperation in such fields as statistics, environment, energy, and related issues. According to the committee it was to be open, and its members would be free to join any other international organization they wished.

This consensus was regarded by many analysts, ourselves among them, as predominantly political in character. In this interpretation, the important issue was abolition of the *CMEA system,* and the problem of the organization was of secondary importance. As the change from the CMEA trading system to hard-currency settlements was a foregone conclusion, establishing a new organization did not seem an essential step. While some of the member countries considered it important to retain the appearance of institutionalized cooperation within the former bloc, others saw no reason to deny them the opportunity for face-saving. Furthermore, it was understood that trade and economic cooperation among the CMEA member countries had never been truly multilateral. Bilateral relationships and agreements, especially between the Soviet Union and each of the smaller partners, had been of decisive importance in shaping the pattern of cooperation, and therefore the integration of the CMEA could have been called *radial.* All this suggested that a new organization would not effectively shape the new system of economic relations within the former CMEA or the means of transition to this new system—that the really important strategic and technical issues would be decided by the partners concerned in a bilateral framework in the post-CMEA period as well.

In spite of the seemingly uncontroversial nature of the issue, the decision was put off more than once. As a result, the CMEA as an organization for the most part survived the system it represented. Eventually, when the final decision concerning the dissolution of the CMEA was made in June 1991, the idea of a new organization was for all practical purposes removed from the agenda as well.

Economic Cooperation Versus Integration

The disinclination for establishing a new organization was a reflection of the political changes that were taking place in the former CMEA countries (including the Soviet Union) and in their interrelationships in 1990 and early 1991. In the light of those changes, the issue of establishing a new organization proved more ambiguous than it had once seemed. Conflicting views with regard to the character of the post-CMEA organization in fact reflected divergent conceptions of post-CMEA economic relations and of the economic and trade strategies to be followed by the former CMEA countries. For example, should the suggested post-CMEA organization include *all* former CMEA countries—in Europe as well as outside it—or be limited to the former European CMEA? Obviously, this seemingly simple question had both political and economic implications. The establishment of an organization comprising all of the countries of the former CMEA, irrespective of geography, level of socioeconomic development, and the nature of their economic problems and policies, could be seen as a largely political act directed at maintaining some version of the former bloc even if very different from its predecessor. Furthermore, the experience of the past ten years or so of the CMEA suggested that what the non-European countries were interested in was preferential treatment *within* the organization. From the point of view of the Central and East European countries, however, preferential systems for the developing countries were the responsibility of other, *global* international political and economic organizations. What is more, preferential treatment for any country within the post-CMEA organization presupposed that the responsibilities of the organization would include trading regimes among its members, and this was something that the reforming Central and East European countries definitely wanted to avoid.

The various concepts developed in 1989–1991 concerning economic relations among the former CMEA countries can be classified in terms of whether the relations envisioned are based on *trade and cooperation* or on some kind of further *integration*. According to some concepts, what is needed is maintenance of trade and good-neighborly political relations that will allow for trade development as soon as the economic and political conditions of the partners permit and cooperation in solving similar problems of reform and systemic transformation. There are, however, other influential views, both in the East and in the West, that call for a kind of further preferential treatment of intraregional trade. The "extended" version of the proposed post-CMEA organization might, under certain circumstances, have come close to this concept, and certainly that is the reason Central and East European countries rejected it. This version is not very far from another idea suggested time and again of a *renewed CMEA* that would be market-driven and open to the world, with preferential treatment in the possible form of a free trade area granted each other by participants. The most popular idea in the West, however, is the establishment of an East European Payments Union (EEPU) modeled to some extent on the postwar European Payments Union. According to its proponents, this would be a multilateral clearing system aimed at assisting the multilateralization of trade among the former CMEA countries and, in the first instance, at easing the financial burden of the shift from ruble to dollar trade.[1]

The problems with these ideas are multifaceted, even apart from those related to the economic and financial consequences of the political disintegration of the Soviet Union. To understand them, one must differentiate between schemes concerning the whole of the European CMEA (including the former Soviet Union) and those involving only a part of it (Central and Eastern Europe or some of the countries of the region). We will return to the latter alternative below; here some brief comments on the version that includes the former Soviet Union are apposite.

Without going into a general critical assessment of the particular projects suggested in the period between 1989 and mid-1991, it should be noted that they explicitly or implicitly presupposed the maintenance of the Soviet Union and its economy as an integrated unit and actor in international economic relations. With the benefit of hindsight, those projects were based on a very optimistic scenario for Soviet economic and political developments: preventing the collapse and stopping the processes of disintegration. As time passed, Soviet disintegration and disruption made plans for (re)integration of Central and Eastern Europe with the Soviet Union more and more impracticable. Finally, in the last months of 1991 it became absolutely clear that what the successor republics of the Soviet Union would have to address in the coming difficult months and years was how to manage their *internal* economic and financial relations (within the former Union) in order to avoid chaos, famine, and economic warfare.[2] Given the continuing economic deterioration, unpredictable political change (involving changes in the status of the present republics and their Commonwealth), and the total lack of the stable institutions necessary for the normal functioning of foreign economic relations, talk of any integration scheme involving Central and Eastern Europe and the former Soviet Union has clearly become irrelevant.

The original idea of the EEPU was that it could ease and manage the burden of transition from the transferable-ruble system to hard-currency settlements and convertibility in Central and Eastern Europe. Partial external (Western) financing of the clearing balances in trade among the former CMEA countries would be instrumental in mitigating the possible balance-of-payments tensions that could arise as a consequence of terms-of-trade losses for the smaller countries. Clearly, the transition to dollar trade has taken place without anything like an EEPU system, and therefore the question in 1991 was whether the scheme might be (theoretically at least) an alternative to existing bilateral trading and financial arrangements. Whether the West (or the Western banking system) would be willing (partially) to finance this scheme is a separate question; as far as we know no one has assumed any such obligation.[3] As is pointed out by Kenen (1991) and Richter (1991), from a technical point of view the problem is that if the traditional pattern of intra-CMEA trade persists and the exchange of Central and East European manufactures for Soviet energy and raw materials continues (which *is* the aim of this particular exercise), the Soviet Union will become a persistent creditor (all the other countries persistent debtors), and this is not a situation that can be handled within the framework of a multilateral clearing system. Most analysts suggest that it is unrealistic to suppose that, given its hard-currency situation and present economic-policy priorities, the Soviet Union would be inclined to participate in the scheme.

For obvious reasons, the Soviets (or, more precisely, the Russians) are compelled to secure the largest possible amount of hard currency revenue from exports (this is why the transferable-ruble trading system was abandoned), and this consideration may in fact lead to their rejecting the idea of the EEPU. There are, however, other important considerations that they should take into account in balancing the pros and cons of this scheme. As has been shown in the previous chapter, the collapse of Soviet imports from the former CMEA countries is an issue of the most serious concern. Therefore, the former Soviet republics (notably Russia, which is responsible for the overwhelming proportion of the oil and other raw material exports) should be interested in addressing simultaneously the issues of hard-currency revenues and domestic commodity shortages. A multilateral clearing scheme might offer the possibility of addressing both problems. For example, excluding most oil deliveries from the clearing scheme (as they effectively were excluded from the indicative lists in 1991) would be a mechanism not only for maintaining effective hard currency receipts for trade with the Central and East European countries but also for increasing imports and avoiding persistent clearing surpluses. In fact, this solution would make the Five persistent creditors of Russia.

This would clearly be an unacceptable solution for the Central and East Europeans. It would not ease trading conditions but make them more difficult than before. As a matter of fact, the Russians, with very few exceptions, simply lack commodities other than oil and some other raw materials for exports, and even oil is becoming scarce. Therefore, Russia's willingness and ability to export oil and other raw materials in the quantities required by the Five within the framework of any clearing scheme would be a *minimum* requirement for their considering the creation of a multilateral payments system including the former Soviet Union. But the important point is that the prerequisites for the survival of that pattern of trade *no longer exist*. This is the most important lesson to be drawn from the history of Soviet–East European trade of the past decade. Therefore, the very foundations for the suggested EEPU are lacking, and the whole idea has become a nonissue.

It should be stressed that it was not simply the eventual political and economic disintegration of the Soviet Union that made these schemes impracticable and, from a Central and East European point of view, even counterproductive. Even under more normal (post-)Soviet conditions they might have had a negative impact on systemic transformation and economic policy. They would have raised hopes in Central and Eastern Europe that the pains of reorientation and restructuring could be avoided and the traditional pattern of exports maintained. As the lessons of 1991 suggest, this was an illusion. The attempt would have resulted not in easing the adjustment process but in postponing the important decisions. In this sense, the idea of new integration would have hindered the emerging reorientation and restructuring; it would have been inconsistent with the Five's basic aim of becoming integrated into a different community, the EC. Moreover, the emergence of any kind of new integration involving Central and Eastern Europe would have encouraged the notion that all the countries of the region, whether reforming or stabilizing their economies or not, should be integrated into Western Europe not one by one (or group by group) as their economic and political development permitted but as a bloc once the conditions for such integration had been established throughout the bloc. This idea is reminiscent of the concept envisioned by the Soviets and certain Westerners some years ago of a "European house" constructed through some kind of bloc-level integration agreement between the EC and the CMEA (once the latter had become a market-based grouping). Needless to say, it would have been inconsistent with everything the Central and East Europeans have recently achieved through political change.

Toward a "Small" Integration?

We have a different view about the urgent need for developing economic cooperation and integration on a bi- and multilateral basis among Central and East European countries, especially those progressing toward a market economy. We have in mind, in the first instance, Poland, Czechoslovakia, and Hungary, but there is no reason that the evolving cooperation should not eventually be extended to Bulgaria and Romania. Although it is not easy to devise a possible cooperation scheme for the Five, what we can think of is free trade, without customs barriers, and some common action in the field of foreign economic relations. Customs did not exist in trade among the Five in the CMEA period (state trading in the CMEA required other tools of regulation); they were established parallel to the shift to dollar-accounted trade and have become an additional factor of trade contraction among them. Common international action could be very useful in effectively representing common needs and aspirations. At a meeting in November 1991 in Cracow and again when signing the association agreements with the EC in December in Brussels (see Chapter 6), the three countries mentioned have declared their aim to conclude free-trade agreements with each other before 30 June 1992 if possible.

At the same time, the current limitations of such a "small" integration should also be mentioned. It was, of course, not only trade with the Soviet Union that collapsed in 1990–1991 but trade *among* the Five. The reasons for the collapse are similar to those for the decline in trade with the Soviets, but there are some specifics that require some interpretation.

Economic crisis is the single most important cause of trade contraction for the Five as a group. With the partial exception of Hungary and Czechoslovakia, the known or estimated quantitative indicators of the depth of the economic recession and the degree of disequilibrium in Central and Eastern Europe (as indicated in Chapter 1) are also very strong. The Central and East European countries are also heavily indebted to the West, and some of them can manage their debts no better than the Soviet Union. Although ungovernability and political chaos are absent or, in the case of some countries, present to a somewhat lesser degree than in the former Soviet Union (and these countries certainly do not face imminent disintegration), these facts alone are responsible for a significant part of what has happened in trade among the Five. Furthermore, deficiencies in managing the transition have constrained trade among them much as their trade with the Soviets has been affected.

At the same time, some basic features of trade among the Five are very different from those of their trade with the Soviet Union. Whereas all of them have given priority to economic relations with their major partner, division of labor *within* Central and Eastern Europe has been very much neglected. Suffice it to say that during the forty years of the CMEA's existence the share of trade with the other four in the total foreign trade of the five countries has remained at about its prewar low level. In 1937, 10.1 percent of their total imports and 10.3 percent of their exports in 1937 were with each other (Tables 5.1 and 5.2). Trade among the Five amounted to 13–17 percent of their trade in the 1970s and most of the 1980s (as compared with a 36–40 percent share for the Soviet Union), even according to official statistics that overestimate ruble-accounted trade relative to hard-currency trade (for the most recent available data, see Tables 5.3 and 5.4). By 1990, the share of trade among the Five must have been reduced to well below 10 percent of their total trade. As for 1991, preliminary Hungarian data reveal that trade with the other four amounted to 5–7 percent of total foreign trade. Because of the relative insignificance of trade among them, what the Five were concerned with in managing the transition was not primarily trade with each other but possible trends in trade with the former Soviet Union and "traditional" Western hard-currency trading partners.

As has been indicated in Chapter 4, the main concern of the Five was the terms-of-trade deterioration that would probably result from the shift to dollar settlements, and trade contraction was considered an additional negative factor. But, as distinct from trade with the Soviet Union, relations among the Five were not seen as involving significant terms-of-trade changes. Such changes were expected in the Soviet trade because of the imbalances of hard and soft goods; as soft goods (relatively overpriced in transferable-ruble-accounted trade) prevailed in the exports of the Five and hard goods in their imports, the change to dollar settlements and international market prices would certainly result in terms-of-trade losses for them. In the trade *among* the Five, however, imports and exports of soft and hard goods were more or less balanced (Table 5.5).

What was left out of this consideration was that without some temporary arrangements aimed at easing the adjustment process, trade in soft goods (manufactures) among the Five might well collapse. They were simply too costly, out-of-date, and poor in quality to compete with imports from the West or the newly industrializing countries. But this is not the whole story. As noted by Richter (1991), "Technical difficulties . . . , mutual distrust and the general aversion of the enterprises and of the population against products from within the region will, most probably, eliminate not only trade of really obsolete products but a substantial part of trade of manufactures of acceptable or good quality as well." It is important to note that the import policies (or practices) of the Five were effectively shaped by their attempts at trade reorientation as well. Because in the short run changing the export market is much more difficult than changing that of imports, these policies not only lead to the contraction of trade among the Five but may contribute to growing balance-of-payments difficulties.

It is in view of this situation that we are suggesting some version of free trade

TABLE 5.1 Geographical Distribution of Exports by the Five in 1937 (percentages of total exports)

	Developed West	Developing Countries	Socialist Countries	Soviet Union	Bulgaria	Czecho-slovakia	Hungary	Poland	Romania	The Five
Bulgaria	82.0	6.1	11.9	0.0	–	5.5	0.8	4.5	0.2	11.1
Czechoslovakia	68.0	18.9	13.1	0.8	0.7	–	1.9	2.6	5.4	10.6
Hungary	80.5	9.9	9.6	0.3	0.4	3.5	–	0.9	4.2	9.0
Poland	81.9	11.2	6.9	0.4	0.7	4.3	0.6	–	0.9	6.4
Romania	73.0	12.2	14.8	0.1	0.8	8.2	4.4	1.1	–	14.4
The Five	74.6	13.8	11.5	0.4	0.6	3.4	1.8	1.6	2.9	10.3

For the sake of comparability with Tables 5.3 and 5.4, country classification reflects the postwar political divisions of the world. Details may not sum to totals because of rounding.

Source: UN Statistical Office, International Monetary Fund, and International Bank for Reconstruction and Development (1953).

TABLE 5.2 Geographical Distribution of Imports by the Five in 1937 (percentages of total imports)

	Developed West	Developing Countries	Socialist Countries	Soviet Union	Bulgaria	Czecho-slovakia	Hungary	Poland	Romania	The Five
Bulgaria	83.2	3.0	13.7	0.0	–	4.9	1.2	4.2	2.9	13.2
Czechoslovakia	68.2	21.6	10.2	1.1	0.9	–	0.2	1.5	2.5	5.0
Hungary	71.1	11.3	17.6	0.0	0.4	6.3	–	1.1	9.8	17.6
Poland	71.2	22.3	6.6	1.1	1.2	3.5	0.6	–	0.7	6.0
Romania	71.8	6.0	22.2	0.1	0.0	16.1	4.1	1.7	–	21.9
The Five	70.8	16.8	12.4	0.7	0.7	4.5	0.9	1.3	2.8	10.1

For the sake of comparability with Tables 5.3 and 5.4, country classification reflects the postwar political divisions of the world. Details may not sum to totals because of rounding.

Source: UN Statistical Office, International Monetary Fund, and International Bank for Reconstruction and Development (1953).

TABLE 5.3 Geographical Distribution of Exports by the Five in 1989 (percentages of total exports)

	Developed West	Developing Countries	Socialist Countries	Soviet Union	Bulgaria	Czecho-slovakia	Hungary	Poland	Romania	The Five
Bulgaria (1988)	6.3	11.4	81.5 (100.0)	62.5 (76.7)	—	4.6 (5.6)	2.0 (2.5)	4.1 (5.0)	2.0 (2.5)	12.8 (15.7)
Czechoslovakia	27.9	16.9	55.5 (100.0)	30.5 (55.0)	2.3 (4.1)	—	4.0 (7.2)	8.5 (15.3)	1.8 (3.2)	16.6 (30.0)
Hungary	43.1	14.2	42.7 (100.0)	25.1 (58.8)	0.7 (1.6)	5.1 (11.9)	—	3.2 (7.5)	1.5 (3.5)	10.4 (24.3)
Poland	48.7	11.5	37.4 (100.0)	20.8 (55.6)	1.6 (4.3)	5.5 (14.7)	1.6 (4.3)	—	1.1 (2.9)	9.8 (26.2)
Romania	27.7	24.1	30.8 (100.0)	17.3 (56.1)	1.3 (4.2)	2.4 (7.7)	2.3 (7.5)	2.1 (6.8)	—	8.0 (26.1)
The Five (1988)	24.0	14.4	61.0 (100.0)	38.1 (62.4)	1.9 (3.1)	3.2 (5.2)	3.0 (4.9)	5.1 (8.4)	1.5 (2.4)	14.8 (24.3)

Because of the overvaluation of the transferable ruble relative to the dollar, trade shares of socialist countries (as a group and for individual countries) are overestimated, but the degree of overestimation is different from one country to another. It is greatest in those countries with the largest shares. The relative shares of the Soviet Union and the Five of trade with socialist countries (in parentheses) are also helpful in assessing the significance of trade among the Five. Details may not sum to totals because of rounding.

Source: UN Monthly Bulletin of Statistics (July 1990); *IMF Direction of Trade Statistics* (1991).

TABLE 5.4 Geographical Distribution of Imports by the Five in 1989 (percentages of total imports)

	Developed West	Developing Countries	Socialist Countries	Soviet Union	Bulgaria	Czecho-slovakia	Hungary	Poland	Romania	The Five
Bulgaria (1988)	15.3	9.3	74.5 (100.0)	53.5 (71.8)	–	5.4 (7.3)	1.9 (2.6)	5.0 (6.7)	2.1 (2.8)	14.3 (19.2)
Czechoslovakia	29.7	13.4	56.6 (100.0)	29.7 (52.5)	2.2 (3.9)	–	4.8 (8.5)	8.6 (15.2)	1.7 (3.0)	17.3 (30.6)
Hungary	49.3	9.9	40.7 (100.0)	22.1 (54.3)	0.9 (2.2)	5.1 (12.5)	–	3.3 (8.1)	1.6 (3.9)	10.9 (26.8)
Poland	53.1	10.6	35.8 (100.0)	18.1 (50.6)	1.2 (3.3)	5.7 (15.9)	1.6 (4.5)	–	1.0 (2.8)	9.6 (26.8)
Romania	10.2	39.9	49.5 (100.0)	28.2 (56.7)	2.3 (4.6)	4.1 (8.3)	2.9 (5.9)	3.6 (7.3)	–	12.9 (26.1)
The Five (1988)	23.4	12.2	59.9 (100.0)	35.4 (59.1)	1.8 (3.0)	3.3 (5.5)	3.0 (5.0)	5.6 (9.3)	1.7 (2.8)	15.5 (25.9)

See Table 5.3.

Source: UN Monthly Bulletin of Statistics (July 1990); *IMF Direction of Trade Statistics* (1991).

TABLE 5.5 Commodity Composition of the Trade of the Smaller CMEA Countries in 1989 (percentages of total exports or imports)

Commodity Class (SITC Code)	Global	Developed West	Developing Countries	Smaller CMEA Countries[a]	Soviet Union
Total Exports					
Food (0, 1, 4)	10.5	13.7	12.8	7.9	7.9
Crude materials excluding fuels (2)	4.4	2.8	6.8	2.4	1.0
Fuels (3)	6.8	12.8	4.6	7.1	0.3
Chemicals (5)	9.9	10.9	17.7	8.5	6.7
Machinery and transport equipment (7)	36.6	15.8	29.2	49.5	53.7
Other manufactures, etc. (6, 8, 9)	31.8	44.0	28.9	24.6	30.4
Total Imports					
Food (0, 1, 4)	6.4	10.4	26.3	7.9	0.4
Crude materials excluding fuels (2)	6.2	6.6	14.3	2.4	5.6
Fuels (3)	26.7	1.9	20.1	7.1	44.5
Chemicals (5)	6.8	16.5	4.9	8.5	2.6
Machinery and transport equipment (7)	26.8	36.9	9.6	49.5	18.7
Other manufactures, etc. (6, 8, 9)	27.1	27.7	24.8	24.6	28.2

[a] The Five and the former GDR.

Source: UN Statistical Yearbook, UN Yearbook of International Trade Statistics, UN Monthly Bulletin of Statistics.

within Central and Eastern Europe. Of course, we think that it is high time to discontinue trade in internationally uncompetitive goods. However, it takes time for industries or firms to become competitive, and we consider it appropriate to try to give *temporary* preferential treatment to each other's exports. As the countries of the region have recently concluded association agreements with the EC providing for free trade within a decade and are negotiating for free trade with the EFTA (see Chapter 6), preferences for trade among the Five would continue for a limited but important period of time. From another point of view, should the Central European countries establish free trade with the EC and the EFTA and *not* enter into free-trade agreements with each other they would sooner or later face de facto discrimination on each other's markets.

Clearly, the limitations of "small" integration are very much the same factors as are responsible for the dramatic trade decline of 1990–1991. First, the deteriorating economic situation and internal and external disequilibria render the change to a market economy difficult in all of the countries of Central and Eastern Europe. Therefore, it is not an easy task to establish market-type integration among them. Second, as has been indicated above, the countries involved are very far from being each other's most important trading partners, and this means that, whereas free trade among them might help to solve some of their economic problems—for example, that of the small domestic markets for some firms or some industries—and to shape the process of *gradual* adjustment to the competitive international environment, it cannot be an integration of a strategic kind. Problems of inward-oriented as opposed to outward-oriented strategies cannot be solved by engaging in this kind of "small" integration. The most important trading partners, commodity markets, potential foreign investors, and sources of technology and external financing will remain outside its scope.[4] Obviously, the relative insignificance of trade among them is a result of the CMEA's pattern of radial integration. This means that change to another type of relationship among them may gradually lead to a more efficient division of labor and more trade. At the same time, the limits of trade development among moderately developed countries should be taken into consideration. All of them are pursuing the development of trade, in the first instance, with the most advanced countries of the world and not with similarly developed regions. Third, establishing some kind of payments union among them would be possible, but it would not play a significant role in solving their major external financial difficulties. Finally, the political difficulties of closer economic cooperation should be taken into consideration as well. The sad fact is that the idea of any Central European integration faces quiet opposition on the part of the governments of the respective countries. For good or bad reasons, all seem to be convinced that integration with their neighbors would not help them to solve their economic problems. At this point, there is even a real danger of disruption of such contacts as exist (for example, in the field of tourism).

"Small" Integration from an International Perspective

It is in the above context that we must consider Western suggestions of a link between Central European intraregional (multilateral) cooperation and the integration of the countries of Central and Eastern Europe into the international economy or the EC. There seems to be a relatively strong school of thought in the West asserting that Western assistance in debt management and promotion of these countries' integration into Europe should be made *conditional* on the progress of intraregional cooperation (Brzezinski 1990).

The attempt to promote Central European cooperation should be welcome. There is no reason whatsoever that countries facing the same or similar problems of socioeconomic development should not cooperate closely. There are strong arguments in favor of further development of economic relations among them, and, of course, it is imperative to try to counteract the deterioration of intraregional political relations. The Central and East European countries should understand that without good-neighborly relations among themselves they cannot enjoy good relations with the western part of the continent.

A related argument in favor of the above-mentioned conditionality is that the West (the EC) should not encourage any kind of "race" for EC membership among the Central European countries, which would endanger intra–Central European relations instead of improving them. On this point we disagree. The problem of joining Europe will be taken up in Chapter 6. Here suffice it to say that there is absolutely nothing to support the belief that rivalry for Western "favors" and acceleration of the process of adjustment to EC rules and regulations in the countries of the region would endanger relations among them. On the contrary, developing institutional relations with the West, adjusting to Western political and legal institutions, and defining the conditions and establishing the eventual timetable for joining the EC would help to shape not only political democracy and market-economy relations in the respective countries but also political and economic relations within Central Europe. Establishing an institution of multilateral economic cooperation is in itself no guarantee of economic and good-neighborly political relations. Most important, if such cooperation were to be established because of Western pressures alone it would be very difficult to avoid concluding that the whole idea of Central European integration was but a convenient way of preventing the Central European countries from becoming integrated into Europe. As politically desirable as closer cooperation among these countries is, it is unrealistic to expect significant changes in the region's economic situation as a result of any conceivable attempt at "small" integration. With this in mind, the stress on the above-mentioned conditionality is difficult to understand.

In contrast to this Western insistence on a kind of regional cooperation in Central and Eastern Europe, in the (pre–August 1991) Soviet Union there were signs of *disapproval* even of embryonic attempts at creating some foundation for such cooperation (Musatov 1991). The Soviets' arguments were mostly political; it was implied that regional groupings like the Hungarian-Polish-Czechoslovakian triangle were harmful and might eventually lead to an anti-Soviet *cordon sanitaire* or Little Entente. Preferential development of bilateral relations with the Soviet Union modeled after Finnish-Soviet relations was suggested instead. To be sure, this emphasis in Soviet policy toward Central and Eastern Europe was a response to what Moscow had every right to consider anti-Soviet tendencies in the policies of some of the new governments in the countries concerned.

However, the Soviets' traditional policy was an insistence on bilateralism in relations with their neighbors and allies and a rejection of any intraregional cooperation that excluded the Soviet Union. Their goal of acquiring the greatest possible bargaining power in their relations with these countries had been the main factor behind the bilateralism that prevailed in the CMEA.[5] If there was a message for both Central and Eastern Europe and the West in those Soviet declarations (and certainly there was), it concerned the importance for the Five of the *political* developments within the Soviet Union. As far as *intentions* are concerned, a victorious conservative comeback would have entailed the most serious consequences for them.

The economic realities are, of course, different. In 1990–1991, Soviet policy toward Central and Eastern Europe was determined by vanishing Soviet economic power and the need for trade reorientation. The collapse of trade relations between the Five and the Soviets was due to Soviet incapabilities and had nothing to do with eventual Central European choices to move toward a (still nonexistent) "small" integration.

Soviet policy toward the Five seems to have changed in the aftermath of the defeat of the August 1991 coup. In government-level declarations in late August and early September, rejection of the evolving Central European cooperation gave way to suggestions that former CMEA member countries should take part in the economic cooperation schemes that would be developed among the former republics of the Soviet Union. This change in attitude can certainly be attributed to various domestic and international political and economic considerations, among them the unexpectedly serious Soviet difficulties related to the shift to dollar settlements. An attempt to make up some of the losses from the trade collapse and revive the inflow of resources from the countries of the region seems to have acquired priority. However, the Five's economic situation and policy preferences and the deep uncertainties involved in the post-Soviet situation preclude the realization of such schemes.

Notes

1. On the concept of the EEPU, see ECE (1990); for a recent critical assessment, see, among others, Kenen (1991) and Csaba (1991b). More recently, the concept has simply been called the "Ecu payments system" (*Financial Times,* 23 April 1991).

2. A multilateral system of cooperation modeled to a large extent after the CMEA is strongly advocated by some widely published proposals concerning economic relations among the former Soviet republics.

3. Although the important thing about the EEPU is that it is a *cheaper version* of the safety net (see Chapter 4) than one financed in the case of each of the Five on a bilateral basis, and this weighs heavily among the implicit arguments in favor of multilateral clearing. It is a significant point of these proposals that the clearinghouse should be established in the West. The Bank for International Settlements in Basel was the first choice for this role, in accordance with the suggestion of the Economic Commission for Europe (ECE 1990).

4. Some Hungarian economists (Lóránt 1990) and sociologists view Central European cooperation as an alternative to a "unilateral" Western orientation of economic policy. This view seems politically and ideologically motivated and not based on economic realities.

5. The logic of rejecting the Common Market (a Soviet policy that predominated from late 1950s until recently) was the same.

6

"Joining Europe": A Thorny Path

"Joining Europe" is among the most intricate issues involved in the Five's policies for the transition. It pertains equally to politics and to economics. "Joining Europe" is at once a trivial slogan for political forces of various stripes in Central and Eastern Europe and a set of strict guidelines for policy action in the field of foreign economic relations. It involves both behavioral patterns in foreign affairs and the creation of a "European" domestic political, social, and economic order, including a market economy with social considerations and multiparty political democracy. In particular, adjustment must be made to the rules and regulations that exist (or will come to exist) in the EC.

In short, "joining Europe" is simply another synonym for "systemic transformation" or "establishing a market economy." It entails the transformation of centrally planned economies once isolated from the international economy (not very long ago they were supposed to constitute a separate "socialist world system" and to participate in an "international socialist division of labor" within the CMEA) into market economies that are an organic part of the world and of the European economy. In this context, the typical Western reminder that Central and Eastern Europe's marriage with Europe will be a protracted process is inconsistent with its emphasis on the need for their swift transition to a market economy.

Opening Up to the World or Joining a Regional Integration?

As regards foreign economic affairs, "joining Europe" is merely the opening up of the former socialist economies. Joining Europe, as seen from Poland or Hungary, is not just joining a dynamic form of *regional* integration (the EC) in place of the defunct CMEA but integration into the *international* economy after forty years of involuntary seclusion. For these countries, Europe is not so much a continent distinct from America or Asia as one of the centers of a global economy previously blocked to them by the CMEA structure. They want to join the world economy, and for geographical reasons they must become part of the EC regional integration to do so; indeed, no other option is available.[1]

Beyond their recent membership in the CMEA or even the Warsaw Pact, the Five have development patterns distinct from those of the countries both to the east and to the west of them. Their economic backwardness dates farther back than the Soviet takeover of the region in 1945, although the degree and type of backwardness varied. (In particular, Central Europe, comprising Poland, Czechoslovakia, and Hungary, falls in a different category from the Balkan states.) In other words, it is not just their recent inclusion in the Soviet bloc that makes them different from the countries of Western Europe and causes them such difficulty in joining Europe. History should not, however, be interpreted as precluding the possibility of overcoming that relative backwardness. Japan, Southeast Asia, and even some countries of southern Europe are recent examples of historically underdeveloped areas remote from the centers of global or European development that have proved able to catch up with the advanced regions, mostly through export-oriented policies. The important message is that overcoming historical backwardness was but wishful thinking and illusion under the autarkic policies of the CMEA. The economic reorientation of the former socialist countries is the single most important condition that makes this goal achievable.

From a different perspective, Central and Eastern Europe have a long tradition of intensive economic, political, and cultural relations with Western Europe that was disrupted after World War II. Trade with Western Europe and specifically with the countries that are now part of the EC was the most significant element of their foreign economic relations, and this will certainly facilitate outward-oriented policies with regard to the EC.

The European Community and the Five: Some Asymmetries

There is consensus in both the East and the West that orientation toward the EC should be a strategic objective of the Five in both political and economic terms. It is with regard to the feasible pace of the rapprochement and its institutional prerequisites and possible outcomes that views conflict.

Although the origins of these disagreements and misunderstandings are various, they must be considered within the framework of the general uncertainty surrounding the new international political situation. The uncertainties of Western policy and the economic and political developments in Central and Eastern Europe (as well as in the former Soviet Union) reinforce each other. As has been argued in Chapter 5, Western attempts at minimizing these uncertainties by approaching the former CMEA countries (or some of them) as a bloc are neither effective nor realistic. A bloc approach would ensure their political and economic disintegration, with all its predictable negative consequences for socioeconomic developments and the political situation in Central and Eastern Europe.

Most important, the EC is institutionally incapable of reciprocating the Five's perception of "joining Europe" as a strategic transformation from isolationism to participation in the world economy. Community action is largely directed by the vested interests of a regional organization and its member states, pressure groups, and bureaucracy. The EC has assumed an important role in the international support for Central European reforms and may help to shape general Western attitudes toward the economies in transition. However, its attitudes toward the applications for membership of Poland, Czechoslovakia, and Hungary have been shaped more by direct commercial interests and policy priorities of its own than by any general considerations with regard to the international repercussions of the dissolution of the Soviet bloc.

Reorientation to the West and the discontinuation of the one-sided Soviet trade of the Central and East European countries had always been regarded as important conditions and goals of systemic transformation, but the 1990–1991 collapse of trade with the Soviet Union dramatically increased the need for reorientation. More precisely, the sharp drop in Soviet (intra-CMEA) trade automatically involved an increase in the proportions of trade shares with other regions, but it is a dynamic growth of trade with countries outside the CMEA that will make it possible to prevent a serious decline in overall Central and East European foreign trade.

The European Community has traditionally been the Five's most important trading region outside the CMEA. In 1989, 25 percent of Hungarian exports and 30 percent of imports were with EC countries. The corresponding data for Poland were 33 percent and 34 percent respectively. The EC proportions of Czechoslovak foreign trade were considerably lower, 18 percent, and the relevant data for Bulgaria were 5 percent and 10 percent respectively.[2] (The proportions of trade with the United States and Japan for all three countries were by comparison almost negligible.) Conversely, the share of the Five in total EC trade was about 1.2 percent for imports and 1.1 percent for exports in 1989.[3] This demonstrates a tremendous asymmetry in mutual dependence. In the aftermath of the collapse of the CMEA, the asymmetry has become even more pronounced. Central and Eastern Europe's prospects for macroeconomic stabilization depend to a large extent on the feasible growth rate of trade with the EC. For the EC or any of its members, development of trade with the Five is generally irrelevant from a macroeconomic point of view. An additional factor pointing to dependence is that whereas for the Five there are few opportunities for finding export markets outside the Community, imports from those countries can be easily replaced from other sources by EC importers.

Association Agreements: On the Way to Joining Europe?

Contrary to the expectations of Central and East Europeans (policy makers and public alike) and the vague promises of some Western governments, they probably will not receive full membership in the Community until well into the next century. What *has* been achieved, however, is a set of bilateral association agreements signed in December 1991 and scheduled to come into force in January 1993,[4] which will replace the EC trade and cooperation agreements signed with Hungary in 1988 and with Poland and Czechoslovakia in 1989.[5] Each agreement is country-specific though based on the same general principles. The association agreements (the EC prefers to call them "European agreements") provide for the gradual introduction over a ten-year transitional period of free trade in manufactures. The transition would take place in an asymmetrical way, with the EC phasing out customs duties and quantitative restrictions faster than its partners. This asymmetry is an important provision for the obvious reason that the Central and East European economies are generally much weaker and need time for adjustment. Further, as has been indicated in earlier chapters, because Poland and Hungary have removed most nontariff barriers to imports virtually overnight without replacing them with a transparent tariff system, their domestic markets are "more open and vulnerable than the EC" (*Financial Times*, (19 April 1991). Textile tariffs will be abolished during the transitional period and steel duties within five years. Quantitative restrictions in "sensitive" areas will also be discontinued. Liberalization in services, capital, and labor is also foreseen by these agreements. Bringing the legal and financial regulations of the partners into conformity with those of the EC is a most important part of the association.[6] Although the agreements include political dialogue, economic cooperation, technical assistance, and financial support, no free trade in the critical area of agriculture is foreseen. Quantitative limits on duty-free imports and levels of duty for a long list of individual products have been agreed upon. The agreements refer to all "four freedoms" of economic integration as stipulated by the Rome Treaty (free trade and free movement of labor, capital, and services), but, as is stressed by Balázs (1992), provisions about the "movement" (without the adjective "free") of workers, establishments, and services "are either uncertain or foresee action only in the rather remote future." At the insistence of the Central European countries, general and nonbinding reference to their accession to the EC as an ultimate though not automatic goal is made in the preambles to the agreements. Clearly, this cannot be interpreted as a firm promise, and no scenarios for preparation for full membership are currently under consideration.

A typical Central European comment (Balázs, 1992, p. 8) is that, although the political content of the agreements is particularly rich (it stipulates consultations at the highest political level, establishes a system of political dialogue, creates an Association Council to supervise the implementation of the agreements, and so on),

> the economic effects . . . are probably less important. Possible short-term trade creating effects and additional advantages for Hungary as compared to the already existing GSP [Generalized System of Preferences] treatment should be analysed. The question is whether the asymmetrical timetable for reaching free trade would

result in asymmetrical trade growth similarly i.e. in favor of Hungary or competitive EC exports to Hungary would progress more rapidly even through a limited market access than Hungarian sales on the EC markets in better trade policy conditions, because of the enormous difference in export potentialities of the two parties. The limited scope of financial aid to Hungary is a spectacular difference between the Hungary-EC agreement and other (e.g. Mediterranean) Association Agreements of the EC.

According to another view, petty bargaining on a technical level (on a commodity-by-commodity basis) has characterized the negotiations on the association and the agreements concluded, and the association agreements lack comprehensive economic and political content.[7]

The reasons that integration of these countries into the EC will be a lengthy process are various. To begin, the EC has priorities other than expansion through the inclusion of the Central and East European countries, and in the opinion of the Brussels Commission those priorities would be endangered by early inclusion of the former socialist countries. The EC's first priority is the completion of the Single Market and a further move toward European union in accordance with the Maastricht decisions of late 1991. Moreover, an important aim is the European Economic Area comprising the EC and the EFTA, although progress in that field is also slow and cumbersome. Frequent reference is made to the long list of applicants for EC membership, ranging from Austria and Turkey to possibly Switzerland and the Scandinavian countries. Countries that applied earlier and have more developed market economies have clear preference over the Central and East European countries. It is often suggested that there are other international political constraints to be taken into account in considering Central European applications; the possibility of Soviet opposition to the accession of the three countries has sometimes been mentioned by EC officials as an example. Whatever the past relevance of these arguments, it is unlikely that in the aftermath of the disintegration of the Soviet Union this will remain a problem.

Further, a series of trade conflicts between the EC or some of its members and the new applicants have arisen in the negotiations for a rapprochement. As do most other Western partners of the Central and East European countries (governments and international organizations), the EC insists on rapid economic liberalization, abolition of governmental subsidies, and so on, in those countries, but it is clearly unwilling to make significant concessions to their broad protectionist policies. It is in those fields in which the Five's exports are relatively significant that Community markets are glutted, and the Commission is unwilling to offer free entry on a competitive basis even though actual or potential trade flows seem to be minimal. The most notorious example is agriculture, where asymmetries are also very pronounced. The share of the Central and East European countries in the Community agricultural imports was 1.6 percent in 1988 while the Community share in agricultural exports of those countries was about

23 percent.[8] Hungary is a large exporter of agricultural products, which represent about 30 percent of its exports to the EC, and 36 percent of its agricultural exports went to the EC in 1990. Hungary sought to become part of the Common Agricultural Policy (CAP) of the EC within the framework of the association, but its request was rejected by the Brussels Commission. The EC has even failed to respond to a Polish proposal for phased liberalization in the agricultural sphere over ten years. It is not only that several of the southern European countries fear being outcompeted in some commodity markets and thus oppose any open-handed trade policy toward Central and Eastern Europe. France also defends its protectionist policies, as was demonstrated in September 1991 when the French veto on meat trade prevented the Foreign Ministers of the EC countries from coming to an agreement on the association of Hungary, Poland, and Czechoslovakia even though acceleration of the process of association was one of the Western promises made to the Central Europeans in the aftermath of the August 1991 coup in the Soviet Union.[9] Agricultural protectionism is, of course, an issue not only of Community relations with the East; the immense agricultural subsidies offered to EC farmers in the framework of the CAP are a bone of contention in its relations with the United States.[10]

A truly difficult situation is evolving. For obvious political reasons and in the absence of alternatives, the governments of Poland, Czechoslovakia, and Hungary have placed great importance on achieving association with the EC as soon as possible, even though from a trade standpoint some of the agreements' stipulations are not clearly favorable. Lacking significant measures for eliminating trade barriers and facilitating critical Central and East European exports to the Community, the global short-term effect of association on their economic performance may not be at all positive, and the implications for transition policies may be very unfavorable.

This is not to say that the elimination of trade barriers is sufficient for export success. In reality, for the majority of commodity categories concerning manufacturing there are no administrative restrictions to their export to the EC. In some commodity groups where restrictions apply, not even the existing quotas can be fully used by the Five for lack of exportables under prevailing market conditions. With regard to agriculture, the extensive concentration on the production of grain and meat, which are frequently too costly and of inferior quality, and the underdevelopment of the specialized production of quality food render it doubtful that Central and East European food exports would be able to survive in a free international trade environment. Domestic industrial and agricultural policies, the development of competitive home markets and well-defined trade promotion policies for Central and Eastern Europe will be the most important determinants of future export prospects. However, in view of these well-known impediments to Central and East European exports to the West and the insignificance of the trade flows from these countries from the EC's perspective, its inflexibility concerning the trade issues seems especially petty.

Agriculture and other trade issues aside, the emergence of noncommunist Central and Eastern Europe, with its potential to attract Western investment, may chip away at some of the conditions on which the Community of the Twelve has been built: "One key attraction of joining the Community, on the part of the poorer countries such as Spain, Portugal and Greece, was the fact that a large transfer of resources and investment could be expected from wealthier countries. . . . A European Sunbelt of new industries was envisioned." In their view, the expected reorientation of funds toward the East "will dry up, to a large degree, the flow of funds to those EC members which had expected such a flow" (Czinkota 1991, pp. 25-26). There is no need to overstate the problem; except for the former GDR, hardly any significant reorientation of funds has yet to occur. It remains clear, however, that Central and East European efforts to join the EC are a sensitive issue for southern Europeans.[11]

It is often argued that the Central and East European economies, with their relative backwardness, their serious macroeconomic imbalances, and the embryonic state of market relations, are unfit for EC membership. The present incompatibility of the legal and financial regulations and behavioral patterns of these economies with those of the EC support this argument. Therefore, it is suggested, the EC would be unable to integrate them into its existing system and the evolving Single Market and, more important, the Central and East European economies would be unable to withstand the competitive conditions of early full membership. In most fields, the firms of these countries would soon be crowded out not only in Western Europe but also in their domestic markets by EC competitors, possibly bringing on a depression and a serious deterioration of their balance of payments.[12] This latter point is a fundamental and powerful argument against immediate and unrestricted EC membership for the three countries according to the present terms. For the Polish or the Hungarian economy, instantaneous and total liberalization via full membership would certainly be a rigorous shock therapy and result in a GDR-type collapse but without the possibility of West German financing.

An equally important argument should, however, be considered. Association agreements may certainly play a role in building the institutions of a market economy in Central and Eastern Europe. Yet the Community has rejected the idea that association necessarily leads to dynamic and radical integration. Therefore, there is nothing in the agreements to suggest that association will have any substantial direct or indirect impact creating and strengthening the conditions for economic stabilization and systemic change for the Five in the short-term. As has been indicated, even some unfavorable short-term macroeconomic effects cannot be excluded. This leads to an important point: The completion of the Single Market as planned will probably result in the dynamic growth and restructuring of the economies of the Twelve. If this happens while the East European recession persists, then the gap separating Central and Eastern Europe from the West will widen, and subsequent efforts at reducing it will become even more desperate. Furthermore, if persistent recession strengthens destabilizing tendencies in the region, the EC will be unable to address such consequences of the dissolution of the Soviet bloc as the civil war in Yugoslavia.

The arguments against a rapid accession of the three Central European countries to the EC are valid, then, only *under prevailing circumstances*. The conditions surrounding their membership are subject to Community priorities and political decisions. After all, political decisions allowed for exceptions to EC rules not long ago that made its southward extension possible. The condition of some southern European economies (e.g., Greece and Portugal) at the time of their accession was not materially better than that of the Central European economies today.

Is There a Solution to the Dilemma?

As a possible solution to the dilemma of the relationship between the EC and its neighbors, its external relations commissioner Frans Andriessen has personally[13] suggested the idea of *affiliate membership:* "The Community could offer the benefits of membership, and the accompanying gains for stability, without weakening its drive toward further integration and without subjecting the fragile structures of new market economies to excessive pressure." Affiliate membership would "provide membership rights and obligations in some areas, while excluding others, at least for a transitional period." As strange as it may seem, even under this scheme Andriessen would exclude affiliate members "from areas such as agriculture" (*Business Europe,* 3 May 1991).

A similar idea of a "two-speed Europe" was suggested by Dominique Moisi and Jacques Rupnik (1991). Their approach is political, contending that

> the East's renascent economies could not survive the fierce competition of Western rules. But the EC is . . . a symbol in Eastern eyes of democracy, prosperity and legitimacy . . . to extend democracy to the entire continent must become the Community *raison d'être.* One cannot choose between enlarging and "deepening" the Community. The two must be linked. . . . A "two-speed" Europe is necessary, to allow an opening to the East. . . .

We are in basic agreement with this line of thinking. It seems appropriate to conclude this chapter on "joining Europe" by stressing two points: Firstly, Central and Eastern Europe's adjustment to Community rules and regulations will inevitably be a protracted process because of factors which make instantaneous economic transformation improbable. However, the EC's protectionist policies are further obstacles on the thorny path to full membership. Second, although the present circumstances of the former CMEA members clearly do not warrant full membership in the EC according to standard practices, this must not be taken as an excuse for not establishing effective cooperation with these countries and helping them to cope with the extremely difficult domestic problems of transition. The association agreements are not an adequate response to these problems.

Systemic transformation cannot be imposed or directed from outside. It can only be the outcome of domestic policies of democratization, marketization, and liberalization. Yet economic trends and political developments in and around Central and Eastern Europe point to the danger of further economic destabilization, increasing social strains, and political conflict that could abort the whole process of transformation. The Yugoslav civil war shows that it is no exaggeration to say that European stability is at stake. It is obvious that excluding Central and Eastern Europe will not protect the EC from the effects of conflicts and crises that may occur there. Here a well-designed "affiliate" or some other kind of membership or any other arrangement that would bring the Central and East European countries *inside* the Community would be an important step for both the EC and the countries involved. Of course, no form of affiliation would substitute for sound domestic policies, but for Central and East European countries within the EC, the latter's impact on events would increase with the credibility of its declarations and policies. Given the difficulties of intercountry relations within Central and Eastern Europe and the uncertainties of their relationship with the Soviet Union, this point is worth highlighting.

Obviously, some meaningful arrangements to ease the economic burden of the Five would be a necessary aspect of any affiliation. Although it should not be seen as an act of charity, its real meaning would be to help to prevent derailment of the transformation process. Therefore affiliation should be approached as a commitment on the part of the EC and the governments concerned to political, social, and economic development in these countries in broad conformity with West European patterns. It remains to be seen whether this idea is anything more than wishful thinking.

Notes

1. The "EFTA option" was until recently considered an alternative. The idea was that EFTA would "invite the reform states in Eastern Europe that meet certain economic conditions to secure for themselves free access to the whole West European market by joining a revitalized EFTA" (Kostrzewa and Schmieding 1989, p. 501). However, the transformations in the region have made the political considerations underlying this option irrelevant. The EFTA has not been revitalized, and its members are on their way to joining the EC. Finally, the EFTA as a regional group has been much smaller and weaker and as a trade partner less important for the Five than the EC, and therefore even opting for the EFTA would have made the EC the effective arbiter of all the strategic issues of the integration of the Central and East European countries into Western Europe. In any case, the establishment of free trade with the EFTA must be regarded as an important part of the trade policies of these countries. Accordingly, free-trade agreements (very similar in content to the trade chapters of the association agreements) with the EFTA are in preparation.

2. Computed from the *UN Monthly Bulletin of Statistics,* July 1991. Methodological problems may explain at least part of the seemingly large difference across countries.

3. Computed from *OECD Statistics of Foreign Trade,* Series A, June 1991. In the case of some member countries, such as Germany, the proportion was considerably

higher, though also insignificant—2.0–2.1 percent. (The corresponding U.S. data are under 0.3 percent for both imports and exports.)

4. Through an interim agreement, the trade provisions of the association agreements will come into force in early 1992.

5. Eventually, this could be the pattern for agreements with Bulgaria and Romania, provided that the political and economic prerequisites for such agreements on the part of these countries are fulfilled. The Soviet Union was not included among the countries that would negotiate association agreements. With the recognition of the Baltic states by the EC in September 1991 it seems that they may be considered possible candidates for later association. Albania is a candidate too. The EC's position on the future association of the successor states of the Soviet Union remains open.

6. This includes company law, accounting practices, corporate taxation, financial services, competition rules, industrial standards, consumer protection, protection of property, and so on.

7. I attribute this point to Éva Havasi.

8. Computed from *OECD Statistics of Foreign Trade*, Series B., 1989, and *UN Monthly Bulletin of Statistics*, May 1991. Lacking other statistical possibilities, data on Central and East European exports to the EC include those of the former GDR.

9. As a matter of fact, the French farmers were protesting five hundred tons(!) of additional meat imports from Central Europe.

10. As Peter Norman (1991) comments, "the proselytizing zeal with which the leading industrialized democracies are spreading their creed of liberalization abroad could yet have profound effects on their own policies." He cites a leading economist of the OECD as saying that "for the first time in economic history, the main impetus for trade liberalization is at present coming not from the industrial countries which profess to accept liberal norms, but rather from countries whose past tradition has been to question or reject them." It is this situation that caused Norman Lamont, the British chancellor of the exchequer, to warn that the industrialized world would face charges of "hypocrisy" if the countries of Central and Eastern Europe were not allowed to trade their way to prosperity. According to Richard Portes, "if we in the Community were as economically rational, flexible, and willing to take difficult adjustment measures as we shall require of Eastern Europe, we would take their transformation into market economies as the final overwhelming reason to dismantle the CAP" (1991, p. 32).

11. They are also a sensitive issue for the countries of the developing world, which fear being assigned a lower priority in EC policies because of its new eastward orientation.

12. Contrary to the widely held view, eventual flooding by imports from the EC is not simply "a self-correcting exchange rate problem" for Central European countries. Of course, a flood of imports is evidence of the overpricing of domestic goods and the cheapness of imports at prevailing exchange rates, but devaluation because of balance-of-trade pressures or to make imports more expensive and import-substitutes cheaper is only a textbook solution. In present-day Central Europe where high inflation and recession persist, significant devaluation of the domestic currency could have serious destabilizing effects.

13. The Community has distanced itself from the idea.

7

Hard-Currency Debt and Western Policy

The term "help" or "assistance" is often used in describing Western attitudes toward systemic transformation in Central and Eastern Europe, and this is undoubtedly justified in many respects; Western economic support for the reforming countries has been greatly appreciated. Significant aid is forthcoming in such fields as the environment, infrastructure, education (involving management and vocational training, foreign language education, and scholarships in Western universities), and the sciences. There have been a number of projects to support the establishment and strengthening of the private sectors of the economies in transition. Emergency food grants and other forms of humanitarian aid have been offered to Poland and other countries (including the former Soviet Union). Western political engagement in the "new democracies" has played a significant role in promoting the takeoff of foreign direct investment in Central and Eastern Europe. A substantial number of trade restrictions on the part of Western countries and the EC have been lifted or eased. Common regulations of Western countries aimed at restricting high-technology exports to the former Soviet bloc in the framework of the Coordinating Committee (Cocom) have been relaxed.

One of the initial and most important projects aimed at assisting Central and Eastern Europe was given the code name PHARE (Poland and Hungary: Assistance in Restructuring Economies). In accordance with decisions made at the G7 economic summit in July 1989, twenty-four OECD countries agreed to support economic restructuring in Poland and Hungary. The total Western commitment to the program has amounted to $21 billion. However, as has been pointed out by analysts of the UN's European Economic Commission, this sum must be viewed in the context of the terms offered. Most of the assistance, including 40 percent of the new credits offered on a commercial basis (and because of high interest rates largely unutilized), was debt-creating. Support that did not create debt amounted to less than $500 million for Hungary and $2.5 billion for Poland. Therefore, "if the present Western policy is continued, it is likely that the financial burden will become even greater unless the aid and the reforms stimulate strong export growth" (Mihályi and Smolik 1991, pp. 215–216).[1]

Deterioration of the Debt Situation

Financial relations between the West and Central and Eastern Europe cannot be assessed in terms of assistance; they are guided by strict commercial and business principles. In this respect, little if anything has changed since systemic transformation began. It follows that all the important indicators of the external financial situation for the Five as a group and for most of the individual countries had already deteriorated significantly in 1990, *prior* to the collapse of trade with the Soviet Union. Not only did total gross debt rise from $80 billion in 1989 to $90 billion and net debt from $70 billion to $80 billion in 1990 but indicators of *relative* indebtedness also worsened (Table 7.1). According to OECD data, net debt/export ratios for the Five increased from 237 percent to 292 percent in one year. Net interest payments as a percentage of exports grew from 21 percent to 28 percent and net interest payments from $6.3 billion to $7.7 billion. The debt-service ratio rose from 43 in 1989 to 50 in 1990. The only favorable indicator was a moderate growth in reserves as a percentage of imports (from 38 percent to 42 percent) largely due to funds raised by the OECD countries to finance the Balcerowicz Plan in Poland. The total current account of the Five went from a surplus of $0.9 billion in 1988 to a deficit of $1.0 billion in 1989 and of $3.2 billion in 1990. The approximate deficit of $7.6 billion in 1991 (Table 7.2) can hardly be reduced in 1992.

In Hungary, for example, the general impression is that creditors have become more rigid, not more generous, in the past two years. This is the position both of commercial banks and other private creditors and of governments and international financial institutions (the IMF), demanding balance-of-payments targets for the countries concerned—essentially, a continuing net resource outflow (a surplus on the noninterest current account) to the West that may reach 6 percent or more of the 1989 GDP in years to come.[2]

For Poland the situation is somewhat different, as is witnessed by the spring 1991 agreement with the Paris Club that forgave part (50 percent in the case of all creditors except for the United States, which was willing to cancel 70 percent) of the country's debt to Western governments. As was indicated in Chapter 1, this agreement should not be perceived as a favor to Poland. It has advantages for both sides: the creditors will be able to collect part of their claims, and the debtor will be able to theoretically manage its debt in the future. (However, as Poland failed to service most of its debt in recent years, in the short run the agreement will actually lead to more, not less, debt-service payments.) Poland has reached separate agreements with all seventeen governments in the wake of its general agreement with the Paris Club, and those governments are expecting it to fulfill the three-year program agreed upon with the IMF as a condition of continuing debt reduction. Poland has, however, failed to comply with most of the performance criteria of that agreement.[3]

Negotiations concerning the reduction of Polish debts to commercial banks

TABLE 7.1 Hard-Currency Debt Indicators, 1989 and 1990

	Gross Debt (billion dollars)		Net Debt (billion dollars)		Net Debt/Export Ratios		Debt-Service Ratio[a]		Reserves as Percentage of Imports		Net Interest Payments as Percentage of Exports	
	1989	1990	1989	1990	1989	1990	1989	1990	1989	1990	1989	1990
Bulgaria	9.1	10.4	8.0	9.8	254	468	48	77	27	20	20	43
Czechoslovakia	7.9	7.9	5.7	6.3	105	111	23	25	43	28	9	10
Hungary	20.6	21.7	19.4	20.3	302	343	49	65	20	28	26	35
Poland	41.4	48.2	37.5	41.8	452	418	76	71	47	91	42	41
Romania	0.6	2.3	−1.2	1.3	−21	38	19	10	53	18	1	1
Total Five	79.6	90.5	69.6	79.6	237	292	43	50	38	42	21	28

[a] All interest and amortization on medium- and long-term debt as a percentage of the year's exports.

Source: OECD (1991b).

TABLE 7.2 Current Account Balances of the Five in Convertible Currencies (billion dollars)

	1988	1989	1990	1991[a]	1992[b]
Bulgaria	−0.8	−1.1	−1.4	−1.5	−1.2
Czechoslovakia	0.1	0.3	−1.1	−0.5	−1.6
Hungary	−0.8	−1.4	0.1	0.0	−0.5
Poland	−0.3	−1.2	0.7	−3.0	−1.0
Romania	2.8	2.5	−1.5	−1.6	−1.0
The Five	0.9	−1.0	−3.2	−7.6	−6.3

[a] OECD estimates.
[b] OECD projections.
Source: OECD (1991d).

(the London Club) are making little progress. Furthermore, the Paris Club agreement has not prevented commercial banks, notably Japanese ones, from proceeding with their withdrawal from Poland. (They effectively blocked $500 million of credit offered to Poland in 1990.) These banks do not appear to be convinced of a forthcoming improvement in the Polish economic situation and the country's ability to service its debt in the future.

The aforementioned should be viewed in the context of commercial banks in the region (OECd 1991b, p. 30):

> while attitudes of OECD governments have become much more supportive [of Eastern Europe], the private markets, particularly commercial banks, have become increasingly skeptical. In 1989–90 it became obvious that fundamental changes in economic and political structures were occurring throughout the region and doubts began to grow that Central and East European governments could master change in a relatively short time-span. In addition to this general unease over political and economic uncertainties, several specific events have further undermined confidence.

In addition to Polish debt reduction these events included the emergence of a large Soviet current-account deficit, a Soviet pattern of payment arrears to external creditors dating to 1990 (or early 1991 at the latest, when the Soviet Union was considered de facto insolvent by Western commercial banks), Bulgaria's suspension of interest and amortization payments on its hard currency debt in March 1990,[4] large discounts on Central and East European debt in secondary markets, and "statements by political figures in some other countries" (obviously in Hungary) that debt relief should be sought.[5] As a result, commercial banks have began to reduce their exposure to the countries of the region (Table 7.3).[6] After an initial increase in spreads and shortening of maturities, syndicated credits and bond issues have given way to more traditional bank-to-bank facilities. In 1990, of all the countries of the region, only Hungary and Czechoslovakia were able to borrow on the international markets ($1 billion

TABLE 7.3 External Positions of East European Countries Vis-à-vis Western Commercial Banks (billion dollars)

End of the Year	Liabilities Total	Liabilities Soviet Union	Liabilities Smaller CMEA	Assets Total	Assets Soviet Union	Assets Smaller CMEA	Net Debt (Liabilities − Assets) Total	Net Debt Soviet Union	Net Debt Smaller CMEA
1984	48.2	16.6	31.6	22.1	11.3	10.8	26.1	5.3	20.8
1985	60.7	22.7	38.0	27.0	13.0	14.0	33.7	9.7	24.0
1986	72.1	29.1	43.0	29.5	14.8	14.7	42.6	14.3	28.3
1987	84.6	33.3	51.3	31.9	14.1	17.8	52.7	19.2	33.5
1988	87.4	36.9	50.5	34.4	15.3	19.1	53.0	21.6	31.4
1989	98.1	44.8	53.3	35.1	14.7	20.4	63.0	30.1	32.9
1990[a]	90.5	50.3	40.2	21.0	8.6	12.4	69.5	41.7	27.8
1991 (June)[a]	78.6	43.8	34.8	16.4	6.5	9.9	62.2	37.3	24.9

[a] The GDR excluded; in June 1990, the liabilities of the GDR vis-à-vis the banks amounted to $16.3 billion and its assets to $9.6 billion.

Source: BIS International Banking and Financial Market Developments, annual issues.

and $0.4 billion respectively), and total borrowing for the region showed a sharp decline as compared with previous years. The banks apparently continue to regard the former European CMEA as a single region or bloc, notwithstanding the political developments and the abandonment of that organization. This approach is to a certain extent understandable; although economic relations among the Five are not really intensive, Soviet insolvency has for all practical purposes become one of the most important factors behind the economic decline of the Five in 1991. However, this approach does exacerbate these countries' external financial problems.

Commercial banks are motivated primarily by business considerations, and the important point is that, despite Western governments' seemingly strong political engagement in Central and Eastern Europe and the evolving widely publicized schemes for assisting the economies in transition both materially and by way of advice, banks remained unpersuaded about the coming recovery or export growth in the region.[7] Their concerns or, more precisely, the policies following from those concerns are an additional source of the growing difficulties in Central and Eastern Europe. The consequences of the withdrawal by commercial banks are being borne mostly by international organizations and not by new official financial sources. This is clearly not the kind of financial situation that was generally expected in 1989. Did something go wrong? And, if so, what was it?

"Marshall Aid" Versus IMF Conditionality

Western governments and international organizations faced with unexpected and massive political change in Central and Eastern Europe had to shape new strategies of economic and financial relations with the countries in transition. Bold new initiatives for financial assistance on the part of the West seemed both necessary and feasible, and the idea of a new "Marshall Plan" was suggested. Some of the arguments in favor of a grand design were mostly political in character; a large-scale recovery program for Central and Eastern Europe was regarded by many writers as the West's necessary investment in the establishment of a new world order. As Robert Hormats (1990, p. 4) has put it,

> Having spent trillions of dollars to contain communism in Europe, the West would make one of the great mistakes in history if it refused to spend the several billions more needed to help countries through this hard period. . . . All of those changes could be jeopardized, and Eastern Europe's new leadership could collapse, if living standards do not quickly improve.[8]

Another perhaps more practical and straightforward approach was based on the obvious inadequacy of conventional debt-management policies for certain heavily indebted countries in Latin America in the 1980s. The history of Latin American debt suggests that, without significant Western engagement, economic stabilization (and therefore systemic change) in similarly indebted Central and East European countries would be impossible.

The idea of large-scale Western engagement in Central and Eastern Europe has never been seriously discussed among the Western governments or within the international financial community itself. (In contrast, a large-scale aid program for the Soviet Union was discussed and rejected in the course of preparations for the London summit in July 1991.) Instead, a different approach to economic and financial relations with these countries has prevailed since the 1989 inauguration of the PHARE Program. It is often claimed that the willingness of Western official sources to provide funds depends on the willingness of Central and East European governments to implement reforms (Husain and Diwan 1991), and this has been demonstrated by the support offered to the Polish program of 1990 and by the (much later) decision of the Paris Club to forgive part of the Polish debt. Reform programs in other countries have also been given financial support not in the form of grants but mostly through debt-creating credits, and in addition the support has been made conditional upon the macroeconomic performance of those countries as stipulated in their agreements with the IMF. Thus financial "assistance" is explicitly subordinated to IMF conditionality, and the issue is no longer aid but a very hard bargain.

Agreements with the IMF are extremely important for the Five's economic policies. Without IMF funds or the support for government policies represented by those agreements, other creditors might also withdraw, and the debt-driven economies of most of the Five would certainly collapse. Notwithstanding the many differences in their external and internal situations, this is certainly true of Poland, Hungary, Bulgaria, and even Romania.[9] What the IMF is mostly concerned with, however, is balance-of-payments financing. New credits are provided in order to enable the recipient countries to finance their outstanding debts. As has been indicated, some countries are capable of servicing their current debts while others are not. The crucial point is that compliance with the agreements does not result in a halt to the decline of living standards. Quite the contrary, it requires the successful implementation of domestic austerity measures. Given the grave economic difficulties of the Five, this approach is equivalent to giving up all hope of accomplishing systemic transformation in Central and Eastern Europe without very significant economic decline, income loss for the population, and social conflict.

Two interrelated arguments are typically advanced to explain why IMF conditionality is the ruling principle of Western financial relations with Central and Eastern Europe. On the one hand, it is asserted that there can be no "free lunch," not to mention anything like a Marshall Plan, because of the emerging global capital shortage. According to Collins and Rodrik (1991, pp 116–117),

> it is extremely unrealistic to assume that much of the financing of these investments [i.e., those needed for raising living standards] will come from the developed mar-

ket economies with the exception of financing for German unification. There are no evident sources for capital flows sufficient to finance large external deficits—and in particular there are no evident sources for large grants. Loans would exacerbate the already-worrisome external debt difficulties of several countries in the region. Most of the needed investments to rebuild physical capital stocks will have to be financed internally.[10]

Even the Western policies of support for economies in transition already adopted may result in a reorientation of financial flows to Central and Eastern Europe from other regions also in need of investment, and this "danger," as it is conceived by some developing countries, already complicates their relationship with the West.[11] The idea of assisting the "new democracies" by raising taxes in Western Europe (or other developed countries) is apparently unpopular, and this is not something that governments would risk vis-à-vis their electorates. The country with the greatest involvement with the former CMEA, Germany, has serious financial commitments with regard to the former GDR that preclude financial assistance to other countries. The United States, the most important source of international political support for the Five, is burdened with the world's largest debt and cannot be as generous now as it was after World War II when the Marshall Plan was launched.

It is also suggested that any kind of moratorium on debt payment must involve the commercial banks, which in many cases are the principal creditors of the Central and East European countries. This factor as well as the issuance in some countries of bonds not subject to rescheduling or forgiveness limit the possibilities of large-scale debt relief.

Lastly, the point is raised that, for governments and banks alike, financial relations with the Five have global implications. More open and liberal policies toward East European debt (not to speak of schemes that do not create debt) would soften their policies toward other parts of the world, with immediate ramifications for the global economic and monetary situation. Thus the usual reference to the relatively limited Central and East European indebtedness compared with global debt and to the relative insignificance of East European financial needs in a global context cannot be taken as a very strong argument in favor of any relief.

On the other hand, it is argued that the Five's capacity to absorb financial inflows is limited and therefore a "free lunch" might have no favorable macroeconomic impact. The hard-currency indebtedness of these countries is attributed in large part to their inability, for system or policy reasons, to absorb the funds they have borrowed abroad. Without the financial and monetary discipline imposed on them by the IMF, the authorities would be unable and unwilling to control the economy: domestic spending, especially for consumption purposes, would rise, and inflation would accelerate and imports soar. At the same time, without constraints on their financial balances there would be less pressure for reorientation and restructuring, and together these would inevitably result in the continuation and deepening of the present crisis: "large public loans from official sources—while helpful in the short-run—run counter to the reform process: they can even reduce the effectiveness of reforms because they favor sectors that fall outside the market sphere." (Husain and Diwan 1991, p. 307).[12]

These are certainly familiar problems and important conclusions for Central and East European economies. For both Poland (in the early and mid-1970s) and Hungary (in the 1970s and mid-1980s) it was the lack of effective constraints on spending that led to debt accumulation and, consequently, to economic crisis. There are, however, some serious inconsistencies in this reasoning. As convincing as the arguments are, they do not mean that stabilization policies of austerity according to IMF prescriptions are certain to succeed. Theories and international experience aside, macroeconomic developments in the Five in the past two years do not suggest that imposed austerity is the way out of economic crisis. Sound macroeconomic policies are, of course, needed, but the danger is that austerity may lead only to more austerity. Even in countries that have succeeded so far in managing their debts, the need for continuing the tremendous outflow of resources makes the prospects for curbing economic decline very dim.

Financial Relations and Policy Priorities

In more general terms, it is safe to say that all the implicit and explicit arguments against a Marshall Plan–type or "free lunch" approach and in favor of the continuation of present policies of external financing of Central and Eastern Europe are convincing. Money is scarce; debtors abound; the developing world is in a desperate state; Western governments must not antagonize the electorates; commercial banks have interests distinct from those of governments; and more money for the Five does not necessarily lead to better economic performance and a smoother transition.

Yet all these statements can be formulated equally soundly in a slightly different manner: Money is scarce, but there is no absolute scarcity; the Five are few, and their eventual debts are but a fraction of the funds available in the global economy and of the budgetary expenditures of the OECD countries; commercial banks in many countries have intimate relationships with their respective governments and listen to the latter's advice—and, even apart from this, their assessment of economic prospects and, in particular, of the credit standing of countries in which their exposure is significant is in fact a function of their assessment of official Western policies toward those countries; more money for Central and East European countries under certain conditions might lead to economic improvement and in all probability would make the most difficult years of economic transition easier to withstand. Clearly, the second set of statements implies a different set of policy requirements and options from the first.

In a word, financial relations are subject to policy priorities. Insistence on the maintenance of (almost) exclusively business-type financial relations with the Five and a marginal role for "assistance" in the field of finance in the aftermath of political change must be considered a political choice. The explanations for this choice may involve some of the fundamental issues of international policy in light of the breakup of the Soviet bloc. But whatever its explanation the choice itself has some important implications concerning the whole process of systemic transformation in Central and Eastern Europe. Effectively, it reflects a more reserved attitude toward systemic transformation than the one that is implied in political declarations and policy recommendations of the major Western governments, international organizations, and experts. Contrary to the generally strong emphasis on the need for change in the Five's internal policies, continuity has remained the guiding principle in the very important field of external economic and financial relations. More important, this policy does *not* allow for rapid economic stabilization and the transition to a market economy and opening to the world market. It is consistent with the EC's decision not to admit Central and East European countries in the foreseeable future, but it is totally inconsistent with all the talk about rapid economic transformation and privatization. This policy aggravates the rigorous austerity imposed throughout the region, and it is austerity that makes it impossible to build the much-needed social safety net, on the one hand, and to encourage savings, investments, and entrepreneurship, those indispensable ingredients of transformation to a non–Third World market economy, on the other.[13] This interrelationship between the pace of transition and Western financial support is clearly suggested by Sachs (1991a, p. 244) in advocating rapid transition *and* Western aid. What is needed, he says,

> is cancellation of most of the debt owed to Western governments and banks. . . . Any attempt to collect more than a small share of . . . these . . . would subject Eastern Europe to financial serfdom for the next generation. The debts should be reduced clearly, not in a long-drawn-out battle. . . . needed is long-term finance for development. The Marshall Plan provided grants, not loans for Europe. Grant aid is again needed, for spending on infrastructure and environmental control.

This has in fact remained wishful thinking. The general mood among Central and East Europeans is that they deserve better from the West. In contrast to the more or less strictly economic approach of the narrative so far, historical and moral considerations are put forward. It is the post–World War II division of the world that underlies the economic weaknesses of the Five, and it was not entirely their fault that they became part of the Soviet bloc. The West has a far greater share of responsibility for Yalta and its aftermath. Conversely, the Five played a considerable role in putting an end to the Yalta system, and this change has brought enormous benefits for the West. What is more, political leaders in Central and Eastern Europe frequently complain that the West has not kept the promises of help that it made to the opposition parties and groups *before* the political change.

Financial and economic relations are guided, however, not by considerations of history or morality but by those of self-interest. The real question is what the stakes are for the West in Central and Eastern Europe and what options are available to its objectives. Possible answers are obscured by the uncertainty of the political changes that have taken place in Central and Eastern Europe since 1989, and this may largely explain the apparent irresolution of Western policy with regard to the region.

The concept of "enormous benefits" for the "West" from the disintegration of the Soviet bloc has a degree of incertitude. Although it is certain that 1989 and 1990 were years of historical triumph for the West, when the global situation changed almost everything that had once been obvious became subject to question. For example, what is the "West," and who is receiving the "benefits" in question? The "West" described as the accumulation of developed market economies and democratic states with similar values, including those concerning the international political order, was always somewhat problematic, but the notion had its relevance with respect to its counterpart the "East," the Soviet bloc. Without the "East," the "West" has lost much of its previous role. The direct impact of changes in the East on the West varied from one country to another. While some countries, notably Germany, obtained immense national political benefits from the dissolution of the Soviet bloc, others did not. This fact will inevitably affect political relationships and power structures in and outside Europe.

There are two important new concerns related to the disintegration of the East that are shared by *all* Western countries and international organizations, and Western policies are effectively based on considerations related to these issues. One is implied in attempts at a kind of bloc approach to the countries of the former East. A clear preference for delay in the Five's integration into the West underlies Western insistence (as reflected in financial and economic policy) that these countries pass through the Purgatory of a painful stabilization *cum* systemic transformation. The other concern is explicit, and it has to do with the possible global destabilizing effects of the collapse of the Soviet bloc. The fear is that economic and political collapse will lead to civil war, nationality clashes, and armed interstate conflict in the former Soviet Union or in Central and Eastern Europe and its environs or even to attempted changes in the political map of Europe that could seriously endanger global stability. The West could hardly avoid being drawn into these conflicts. The single most important fact to bear in mind regarding the international significance of Central and Eastern Europe is perhaps not that it marked the boundary between East and West during the cold war but that both World Wars originated in regional conflicts within or involving this region. It is also worth underlining that the attempts at nonengagement of the Anglo-Saxon powers and France in what seemed a regional Central European conflict and their effective acceptance of the *Anschluss* and the occupation of the Sudeten by Germany did not prevent but in fact precipitated the outbreak of World War II.

The Five's Place: Inside Europe or at Arm's Length?

There seem to be no ready-made recipes for fighting destabilization. Economic crisis and popular suffering may easily lead to political destabilization, but these may be overshadowed by ethnic, national, and religious conflicts that are deeply rooted in history. As the Yugoslav experience of 1991 seems to suggest, in the later stages of these conflicts the chances for a political solution are extremely slight.

The greatest danger of destabilization in Central and Eastern Europe lies in the former Soviet Union. Before the aborted coup in August 1991 it was clear that the terrible state of the Soviet economy and the serious political conflict in the country would make it *theoretically* almost impossible to work out a feasible scenario for political stabilization in the framework of democratization and economic recovery. There was a strong perception both in the West and in the Soviet Union that in such a situation any large-scale Western financial and economic engagement in the Soviet Union would in all likelihood prove counterproductive—that is, that it would yield no economic results while at the same time the West would "find itself enmeshed in Soviet internal politics" (*Financial Times*, 11 July 1991). Indeed, the West was convinced that the survival of Gorbachev-style leadership and the unity of the Soviet Union was in its vital interest. The Soviet government of President Gorbachev was, however, no longer in a position (in fact, no one was) to guarantee that Western aid would prevent disintegration.[14] Nor could the West guarantee that any economic reform program that it advised and backed as a condition for aid would work. Therefore, in spite of obvious Western political support for Gorbachev and a clear willingness on the part of leading Western governments to help the Soviet internal situation, the powers present at the London summit refused to accept the joint Harvard-Soviet "Window of Opportunity" plan for large-scale Western assistance in exchange for Soviet economic transformation.[15] Despite the tremendous changes that have taken place in the last six months, including the defeat of the August coup, the end of Gorbachev's presidency, and the disintegration of the Union itself, Western attitudes concerning financial assistance have not changed materially except for the initiation of humanitarian aid.

Whatever the events that unfold in the former Soviet Union in view of these most recent developments, the global stakes in preserving stability in Central and Eastern Europe are higher than ever. Given geographical proximity, difficult political relationships, and the intensive economic ties of the recent past, as well as the uncertain internal consequences of the post-Soviet political situation, this should be understood as a crucial point for Western engagement in Central and Eastern Europe.

The Five, in turn, have their own potential for destabilization. In Poland and Hungary, further economic deterioration could lead to political destabilization.

In the other countries of the region (Czechoslovakia, Romania, Bulgaria, and, of course, neighboring Yugoslavia) nationality clashes or conflict between the member republics of the federations (Czechoslovakia and Yugoslavia) cause the most serious concern. What is more, domestic conflict and disintegration in these countries may have a direct destabilizing effect on the whole region because of its ethnic makeup (especially the existence of large Hungarian minorities in Romania, Yugoslavia, and Czechoslovakia) and the obsolete and simplistic nationalistic endeavors on the part of more than one government in Central and Eastern Europe.

Western attitudes toward the Five are obviously influenced not only by the latter's classification as countries that have left the Soviet bloc and the CMEA and as economies in transition to a market economy but also by their being controversial partners that must be persuaded not to take any steps that would endanger the status quo in the region. In turn, economic and political difficulties and unneighborly relations among these countries might foster authoritarianism, yet another possible source of destabilization.

This situation clearly involves a complicated set of policies for the Western countries. The simple approaches that prevailed up to 1989 are no longer applicable. Earlier, the single most important criterion for defining Western policy toward any country in Central and Eastern Europe was whether (and to what degree) its policies were different from Soviet ones (more reform-minded, more open, or simply challenging). Divergence was rewarded, compliance punished. Today these criteria for using the carrot and the stick do not hold.

Western governments and international organizations apparently believe that stabilization can best be served by keeping Central and Eastern Europe at arm's length. Certainly it would be highly inconvenient and costly for the West to treat the very complicated economic and political problems of Central and East European countries as internal problems of its own. But whatever the arguments for present Western policy, a strong case can be made that it is counterproductive. Most important, holding Central and Eastern Europe at arm's length ensures that the dangers of destabilization will persist in a region very close to Western Europe. Without letting Central and Eastern Europe in, the West will lack effective means for maintaining stability in that region.

Notes

1. Further points to be borne in mind with regard to the PHARE Program are that "one-third of the new commitments (5.2 billion dollars) is in the form of investment and credit guarantees. While these are important for the promotion of resource flow, they will not be activated unless the recipient countries fail to meet their contractual obligations. Much of the total financial commitment is to specific projects and will be disbursed over several years. . . . Credits—and sometimes even grants—offered . . . are frequently targeted to encourage their own companies and various non-profit institutions (e.g. uni-

versities) to invest in or provide services to H-P [Hungary and Poland]. In this case the monetary value of direct gains for the recipient country is only a fraction of the figure entered in the expenditure book of the donor government" (Mihályi and Smolik, 1991, p. 215)

2. According to estimates based on the existing understanding between the Hungarian government and the IMF, Hungary will have to make annual foreign debt-service payments of $3.5–4 billion (13–15 percent of the country's GDP in 1989), of which some $1.6 billion (6 percent of the 1989 GDP) is interest. In view of the significant drop of the GDP in 1990–1991, debt service as a proportion of current GDP in the years to come will be even larger (Köves and Oblath 1991).

3. According to press reports, by late July 1991 the United States was the only country to have signed a pact reducing Polish debt to it (by 46 percent, with a further 20 percent reduction to follow in 1994 provided Poland had fulfilled its IMF agreement.)

4. It was not until February 1991 that Bulgaria reached an agreement with the IMF on an austerity program supported by financing totaling more than $600 million (ECE 1991b, p. 102).

5. Those statements were immediately refuted by the Hungarian government and the National Bank of Hungary.

6. Total net debt of the smaller CMEA countries vis-à-vis the Western commercial banks increased somewhat between 1984 and 1989, but the experiences of individual countries varied; the GDR did not raise new credits for most of that period, Romania was repaying its debt, and Poland was unable to obtain new credits. Bulgaria (up to 1990), Czechoslovakia, and Hungary (also in 1990), however, were in a position to refinance their debts. Essentially this means that the withdrawal of commercial banks from Central and Eastern Europe is a very recent development.

7. According to the *UN Economic Survey of Europe* for 1990–1991, banks have not been very enthusiastic about the political change in Central and Eastern Europe, perceiving the movement toward democracy as something which "raised questions about the authorities' capability to implement strong adjustment measures to control external imbalances" (ECE 1991b, p. 94). This is a strange perception indeed. First, history suggests that lack of democracy in traditional Soviet-type societies had not resulted in the effective control of external imbalances (Köves 1985, p. 134). Second, the experience of the years 1990 and 1991 shows that the real cause for concern is not that the new governments may be unwilling to resort to "strong" measures but that those measures may be ineffective.

8. Various suggestions as to the practicability of a new "Marshall Plan" have been published. Most of them have involved assistance in financial stabilization, a moratorium on principal and interest on debts, and a broader long-term program involving the establishment of a specialized institution "to become the focal point of economic assistance" and the promotion of economic cooperation or even "obligatory" cooperation among Central and East European countries (Rohatyn 1989, Berend 1991). Some of these proposals are soon to be realized, although in a different context. The new London-based European Bank for Reconstruction and Development (EBRD) is a specialized bank established to invest in transition in Eastern Europe but with limited funds and responsibilities. Initially, it is expected to cooperate and cofinance projects with other multilateral institutions, especially in such areas as infrastructure, privatization, reform of the financial sector, and industrial restructuring. Just as Marshall aid was followed by the establishment of the European Payments Union, suggestions of a new "Marshall Plan" involved

Hard-Currency Debt and Western Policy 117

the creation of an East European Payments Union (mentioned in Chapter 5), but the various proposals have not made clear the eventual degree of Western financial engagement in the scheme. Little progress has been made concerning economic cooperation among the Central and East European countries. Here and in the following, the term "Marshall Plan" will be used for any large-scale recovery program for Central and Eastern Europe involving Western financial support.

9. The spring 1991 agreement between Romania and the IMF covers over $1 billion in credit as compared with the $3 billion that the Romanians would need (KOPINT-DATORG, 1991b, p. 9).

10. An illustration of the uncertainties and inconsistencies involved in this argumentation may be found in a leading British newspaper's comments on the possibilities of a "grand bargain" between the Soviet Union and the West on the eve of the July 1991 London summit: "The West spends at least 250 billion dollars a year defending itself against the Soviet Union. It is also closely concerned with the possible fate of the Soviet arsenal. But the case for Western engagement is not merely negative. Economically, the West must welcome so important an addition to the world economy, just as, politically, it would have to embrace so noteworthy an addition to the societies committed to its fundamental values.

"The suggestion of the Yavlinski program *that total assistance should be 0.6 per cent of the annual gross domestic product of the OECD countries over four years (about 100 billion dollars in current prices) is not unreasonable in itself* [our italics]. Provided such assistance is not at the expense of equally meritorious recipients, notably those of eastern and central Europe, the cost is not large, set against the potential gain" (*Financial Times*, 11 July 1991).

11. Competition between Central and Eastern Europe and the developing countries should be viewed, according to the director general of the Organization of Petroleum Exporting Countries (OPEC) Fund, in the context of diminishing official aid, financial funds, and foreign direct investment flows from the West to the developing world: "High and rising interest rates have compounded debt servicing burdens, seriously impairing payment capacities, while commercial banks remain reluctant to participate in fresh packages that require new money. Indeed, the severe drop in net private financial flows, combined with rising interest rates, had led to increased net transfers from the developing world to the North. These net transfers have jumped . . . to 8.2 billion dollars in 1989 . . . It would be tragic to pay reduced attention to the economic decline in Africa, the growing poverty of Asia and the crippling indebtedness of Latin America as we organize to assist less distressed Eastern Europe" (Abdulai 1990, p. 2). True, there is nothing to suggest that these unfortunate trends in South-North (West) relationships relate to the opening of the East. What is more, as Albert Hirschman remarks (1990, p. 20), the perception that events in the East are "surely bad" for the developing world "is dictated by a primitive zero-sum model of the social world: anything 'good' must have a 'bad' equivalent somewhere else . . . the Third World will suffer because a large share of supposedly limited amounts of Western capital, entrepreneurship, and more generally, attention will flow to . . . Central and Eastern Europe." As a matter of fact, the end of the cold war may have a very favorable impact on the developing countries.

12. Efforts are made to support this kind of argument by a reinterpretation of economic history. According to Kostrzewa, Nunnenkamp, and Schmieding (1990, p. 46), "The Marshall Plan for Western Europe after World War II provides an example that

external financing may even retard rather than promote economic reforms. It relieved European governments of the need to correct misguided policies in a way which would have made their countries attractive for private capital inflows. . . ." More to the point is that "the example of development aid granted to Third World economies shows that the lack of capital is typically not the critical bottleneck towards economic progress. Both donors and recipients have to accept that aid flows of whatever magnitude cannot substitute for sound macroeconomic management, undistorted policy incentives, and an adequate institutional framework."

13. The Asian newly industrializing countries are not Third World countries in this respect. As the former vice-president of the Asian Development Bank explains, what "East Europe should learn from Asia . . . is . . . that it is possible to achieve market-driven economic restructuring without incurring unacceptably high economic and social costs" (Katz 1991, p. 15).

14. "The Government of President Gorbachev . . . does not possess the institutional framework either of the market or, nowadays, even of effective government; it has exacerbated macroeconomic instability, not diminished it; it has consistently chosen partial over comprehensive reform; and it has shirked bringing to its own attention let alone to that of the people, the realities of the required revolution" (*Financial Times*, 11 July 1991).

15. Mostly vague promises were offered instead. Concerning the single most important point—the granting of special status with the IMF and the World Bank to the Soviet Union—the Soviets disagreed; they insisted on full membership in those international financial organizations which in turn, as a short-term aim, was unacceptable to the Western powers. Besides, "all international institutions were being asked to work closely together to intensify efforts to support the Soviet Union with advice and expertise to help it create a market economy . . . the G7 could help work for price decontrol and privatization . . . the need to intensify technical assistance particularly in energy, converting defence industries to civilian output, food distribution and nuclear safety was recommended . . . [and] efforts would be made to promote trade" (*Financial Times*, 18 July 1991).

8
Outlook for the Five: External Constraints and Policy Options

For most of 1991, the governments of the Five perceived that year as the lowest point in their post-1989 economic history. They hoped that 1992 would signal the start of a recovery that could lead to perceptible economic growth and an improvement in living standards. Some important economic realities and policy considerations seemed to justify this hope. It was obvious that the enormous external shock caused by the collapse of trade with the Soviet Union could not occur again. Furthermore, most of the dramatic domestic adjustments that cut domestic demand had already been carried out or had begun throughout the region (currency devaluation, often allowing internal convertibility of the respective currencies, price liberalization or official price increases, reduction in consumer and producer subsidies, a general tightening of fiscal policies, the introduction of monetary austerity, an end to job security, and so on).

As 1991 reached its end, it became clear that the worst was not over. Even if there were no additional external shocks, recovery from the collapse of trade with the Soviet Union would depend on the progress of economic restructuring and reorientation, which in turn was a function of both appropriate macroeconomic policies and micro-adjustments in an environment conducive to change. Significant steps toward macroeconomic stabilization and liberalization and important changes in the way the economies of the Five function have already occurred, but all the available evidence suggests that the forces of economic destabilization remain strong. Stubborn inflationary pressures all over the region are one of the most telling examples. Disinflation remains the number one priority of the economic policies of all of these countries. Further severe monetary and financial restrictions are needed even to attempt to hold inflation to its present rate, let alone to reduce it.

External financing problems continue to be very serious. From the outset it was assumed that 1992 would be (at least) the third consecutive year of considerable economic decline and industrial recession in Central and Eastern Europe. A new wave of unemployment is foreseen throughout the region. What is more, "it is impossible to predict with certainty when the turn-around can be expected" (OECD 1991d, p. 57). According to the OECD's fairly optimistic forecast,

> for Hungary the trough may have been reached by mid 1992. Czechoslovakia could lag somewhat behind (though with better inflation performance) and Bulgaria and Romania still more so. For Poland, roughly unchanged output is projected for the next year [1992], though risks of substantially worse outcomes cannot be ruled out. The margins of uncertainty in all cases are of course very large, and issues of political sustainability, which have clearly surfaced in Poland, may pose problems more generally if a turn-around is much delayed.

Policy declarations by the new Polish government of Prime Minister Olszewski make this warning most topical.

Given the external and internal constraints, the feasible short-term task for Central and East European governments is not so much recovery as maintaining control of economic processes. This will not be enough to achieve recovery, but it is indispensable for keeping open the possibility of halting decline and disruption in the foreseeable future. In the very important field of foreign economic relations, "control" is maintaining solvency or complying with the balance-of-payments provisions of agreements with the IMF. The case of Hungary, as one of the relatively most successful examples of debt management in the region, is witness to the enormous dilemmas involved in debt reduction policies. What follows is a mirror reflection of the implications for Western policy reported in Chapter 7.

Debt Management and Transformation in Hungary

"Successful" debt management according to the provisions of the IMF does not, as has been explained, guarantee any recovery from the recession but does manage to provide an important framework for controlling debt. Lack of an IMF agreement or noncompliance with the terms of an existing one may lead to loss of credibility and to debt rescheduling due to default.[1] Nevertheless, extensive discussion of possible policies of external financing has recently evolved in Hungary,[2] focusing not so much on short-term policy options or even one-sided action as on the feasibility and meaning of different strategies for managing the country's large hard-currency debt. The clear majority view in Hungary, shared by the government, the opposition, and most experts, is that to keep the economy afloat it is imperative to continue to honor debt-service obligations. In short, present government policies rest on two arguments: that because of external conditions Hungary has no alternative to servicing its debt (i.e., has no chance of obtaining debt relief) and that it must avoid default and rescheduling.[3] The latter point is supported by general economic considerations and by the grim experience of countries recently forced to ask for debt rescheduling (Eichengreen and Portes 1989). The former is based on Hungary's own experience in the period following political change, which makes it clear that hopes of obtaining Western aid are illusory. This reasoning suggests—explicitly or sometimes implicitly— that for the Hungarian economy there is no need to ease the debt burden. Without the disciplinary effects of the conditions imposed by the IMF, the country would be unable to implement much-needed restrictive monetary policies, cuts in expenditures, and inflationary controls and undertake economic restructuring. The government's tendency to spend more on restitution to prenationalization and precollectivization owners, on subsidies, and on maintaining and expanding its own bureaucracy must somehow be contained, and external pressures can effectively do at least a part of the job.

Independent of such forceful arguments, developments relating to the current balance of 1991 seem to testify that the Hungarian economy is manageable—at least for the time being—despite a net outflow of resources. This leads to the conclusion that this is not the moment to raise the issue of debt relief. The relatively significant influx of foreign direct investment in 1990 and 1991 (Chapter 3) indicates that future balance-of-payments targets may be more easily achieved.

Thus both policy considerations and the experiences of the most recent past suggest that the main policy line of the government and the National Bank should be to continue managing the debt in order to avoid debt relief. It is essential, however, that they prepare the way for a different policy in the event that this one can no longer be pursued or proves ineffective.

The Hungarian balance-of-payments situation has been unstable since at least 1982 (see Chapter 1). During this time the National Bank of Hungary has made tremendous efforts to produce the resources necessary for financing the balance. Nevertheless, under certain circumstances the continuity of this financing might be endangered in the future, partly because in many respects international conditions are unfavorable for Hungary's debt management. As has previously been argued, the entire former CMEA has been struggling with serious financial difficulties, and despite the political developments of the past few years creditors are inclined to treat the whole region as a bloc.

Contrary to expectations, preliminary data show Hungary's current account in convertible currencies in 1991 to be approximately in balance. As this happened despite the collapse of its ruble trade, keeping the trade deficit modest is accurately regarded as a great success, and this is attributable to dynamic growth of exports (although less rapid than that of imports) in Western markets.[4] Given that a large part of the hard-currency export growth in 1991 was directly related to the discontinuation of ruble exports stemming from the shift to dollar trade with former CMEA countries, the scope for further hard-currency export growth under a domestic recession is debatable. The prospects are also uncertain for other current-account items (such as changes in the balances of foreign-exchange accounts of Hungarian households in domestic banks) that have contributed significantly to the positive development of the balance of payments in 1991.

What is more, balance-of-payments financing might be threatened by further accumulation of internal economic and social tensions that arise in part from other sources. Here the problem is not simply that society's capacity for bearing burdens is limited and overstepping these limits increases the risk of destabilization but that, given the nature of things, one cannot tell where the limits are and how they will change in the course of time. Therefore, one cannot know in advance how much prices will rise and in what fields, what the level of unemployment will be, or which economic policy measures will confront sufficient popular opposition to force the government to revise them and make it impossible for it to achieve its balance-of-payments targets.

It follows that even with the improvement of its external financial situation in 1991 one cannot entirely exclude the possibility that Hungary may someday be forced to change its debt-servicing policies. Western decision makers (governments, international financial institutions, commercial banks) do not currently favor the easing of Hungary's debt. This is, of course, in part a consequence of their general policies with regard to financial and economic relations with the countries of Central and Eastern Europe. As has already been demonstrated, these policies must be traced to powerful political and economic considerations.

At the same time, Western policies that base financial relations with the Five on IMF conditionality do not exclude some diversity and versatility in approaches to the varied and changing conditions of individual countries—witness the agreement between Poland and its official creditors to cancel part of its debt. Notwithstanding the various controversies concerning the Polish agreement with the Paris Club (notably the uncertainties concerning its realization and its effects on the Polish economy), it should be regarded as a new approach by Western governments that may also have an effect on Hungarian debt management. It has become evident that creditors are capable of accepting the consistently represented and specific positions of certain indebted Central and East European countries and that, contrary to popular belief, they may be willing to cancel some of the debts of countries other than those in famine-stricken Africa. The idea of any broad departure from current Western financial and economic policies toward Central and Eastern Europe should be rejected as wishful thinking; it is in the context of the most recent developments in the former Soviet Union that the debt-management problems of the Five (Hungary included) should be evaluated. Whatever the short-run scenario of events in the former Soviet Union and its longer-term implications, they do place the danger of destabilization in Central and Eastern Europe and the need to counteract it in a new light. These events, including not only the "end of communism" and of Gorbachev's perestroika but the increasing uncertainty as to what will emerge to replace the Soviet Union, fundamentally increase the significance attached to the achievement and maintenance of stability in Central and Eastern Europe.

In view of what has just been said, it would be untimely to recommend that the Hungarian government depart from the line it is currently pursuing. Additionally, however, it should be made clear to the West that no lasting stability can be ensured in Hungary (or anywhere in the region) without a significant Western commitment or at least the prevention of a net outflow of resources from these countries. It is possible for this position to be represented in a credible way, without risking a loss of confidence on the part of creditors, to the Western governments whose political decisions significantly influence business decisions and attitudes.

Similar ways of thinking concerning the enormous debt burden and the consequent difficulty of economic recovery have given rise to various proposals for future debt management in Hungary. For example, one proposal suggests transferring in the next five years a significant share (approximately 80 percent) of the payments for interest due annually into a "modernization fund" that would be used not for budgetary purposes, subsidies, or consumption but for *development within* the country (Inotai and Patai 1991). According to estimates, such a fund could provide an additional $6 billion to the Hungarian economy, yielding an additional growth rate of 4 percent.[5] Others suggest reducing debt service temporarily to finance special development funds. All these measures would be implemented in cooperation with creditors.

Whatever the merits and drawbacks of particular schemes, debt management is the crux of the matter. The aforementioned problems are specific to Hungary, as the problems of debt renegotiation are specific to the Polish case, but in both cases they have broad implications for the Five. Two points concerning the Hungarian debt management problems just presented should be stressed here.

First, what is involved here is a gradualist approach to managing systemic transformation. The dangers of this approach are twofold. On the one hand, default would inevitably lead to shock therapy—significant new short-term reduction in production and incomes—and with it the most uncertain prospects for the economy and society as a whole. On the other hand, even if default and rescheduling could be avoided for some time, the growing burden of debt service would result in loss of income and decline in living standards. In the latter case, beyond a certain point servicing the debt would lose its economic and political sense; it would lead to a Third World scenario, not democracy or a market economy.[6] Indeed, the end results of the two scenarios are not very different.

Second, because of Hungary's thus far immaculate record of debt servicing, its dilemmas are unique among the countries of the region (Czechoslovakia has a similar history but lacks the present severe debt management problems). The same can be said of the close relationship between debt management and the maintenance of the country's basic gradualist philosophy of economic transformation. Yet it is apparent that dilemmas with regard to debt management are prevalent throughout the region. Because of the policies of their partners, most of these countries face shortages of external financial resources. The most indebted ones have no alternative but a net outflow of resources, even in the long run. Concurrently, economic history and theory suggest that in a period of deep transformation and restructuring a net inflow of resources is needed. Therefore it is no wonder that the policies imposed on them threaten to become impractical or counterproductive.

The Five and the End of the Soviet Union

The most troublesome issue for Central and Eastern Europe is the course of events in the former Soviet Union following the aborted August coup and the disintegration of the Union. The triumph of the conservative forces in the Soviet Union would certainly have meant further destabilization in Central and Eastern Europe. Because of the unavoidable balance-of-payments crisis and the collapse of production in the Soviet Union, not even greatly reduced trade levels could have been maintained. The commercial banks' reaction to these events could have been fatal for at least some of the Five. More important, if the August coup had led to civil war, armed conflicts, and large-scale flight of Soviet citizens abroad ("abroad," for simple geographical reasons as well as because of the relatively intensive relationships of the recent past, meaning primarily to Poland, Hungary, and Czechoslovakia), there would have been danger of involvement of Central and Eastern Europe in Soviet internal strifes. Whether these difficulties could have been counterbalanced by more straightforward Western engagement in the region is open to debate.

This time new shocks were averted, and this in itself is very important for the feasibility of the transition for Central and Eastern Europe. Yet the defeat of the putsch did *not* mean that the difficulties of Soviet–East European economic relations related to Soviet economic decline and political crisis had been overcome or could be easily resolved. The developments of late 1991 and early 1992 have dispelled any illusion of a soft landing for the post-Soviet economy following the "end of communism." The experience of Central and Eastern Europe shows that whereas political opposition to change can be destroyed overnight, the most difficult part of economic and social transformation comes *after* the political reshuffle. The large size and the dire state of the Soviet economy as well as the tremendous political problems related to the discontinuation of the ancien régime and the Soviet state render systemic change in this country much more difficult than in the Five. For example, the most important economic problems related to the end of the Union and the creation of the new Commonwealth of Independent States, including those of the monetary system, trade regimes among the constituent republics, and foreign economic relations, involving among other things the external debt of the former Soviet Union, have remained unresolved. Political problems such as the future of the former Soviet military forces and territorial disputes among and within the new states are the most problematic. It may well be that conflicts *among* the new states (mostly with Russia on one side and the others on the other) will replace antagonisms between the Union and the republics. Political and economic scenarios may vary, but a protracted period of further disintegration and bitter conflict among the actors of post-Soviet history appears inevitable before a politically stable framework and a normally functioning economic system (or *differently* functioning *systems*) emerge.

Following a whole series of economic reform schemes that had failed to materialize, the Russian government of President Boris Yeltsin launched a radical reform program in January 1992. The scheme, called the Gaidar Plan, accepted the most important features of Polish-type shock therapy, including instantaneous liberalization of domestic prices and the introduction of currency convertibility (Sachs 1992, Gaidar 1992). Obviously, those who fashioned the plan took as their starting point the similarity between Soviet and Polish economic problems and especially the analogy between the post-Soviet situation in late 1991 and the state of the Polish economy before the introduction of the Balcerowicz Plan at the end of 1989. Monetary overhang, impending hyperinflation, and default on external debt were common features of the prereform Polish and Russian economies. Although by now it is clear (see Chapter 1) that the Polish shock therapy cannot be considered successful, this fact seems to have been overlooked in shaping the Russian reform scheme. A plausible explanation is that although the prospects for the Polish economy remain uncertain, the Balcerowicz Plan was undeniably successful in ending the shortage economy and hyperinflation with a bold policy of stabilization surgery. In view of the extraordinary and widespread shortages, any reform ideas in Russia must be anchored in a scheme that effectively eliminates monetary overhang.

What had worked in Poland, however, apparently did *not* work in Russia. The shortages there seem to have been much more severe than in Poland, and the whole reform was discredited by the fact that goods remained as scarce after their prices had tripled as before. Moreover, this fact is witness to both domestic reform mismanagement and a lack of much-needed Western engagement in stabilization (e.g., the failure to stockpile the commodities in greatest demand prior to price liberalization, in large part due to a lack of imported goods, and the failure to introduce tight-money policies). A more thorough analysis of how the economies of Russia and other successor states might be reformed is clearly beyond the scope of this book. What seems to be the case is that the differences between Russia and Poland (or other Central and East European countries) are even deeper than the differing extents of shortage suggest.

An additional point to consider is that in the former Soviet Union the old system of mandatory planning (renamed "state orders") survived for all practical purposes until the very end of the Soviet state even though it was no longer really functioning. This was an important handicap to reform; even the Polish economy had gone through a whole series of (albeit inconsistent) reforms by the time of the political change in 1989.

Related to economic reform is the other opaque area: Western policy. To be sure, the complete denial of economic support to the Soviet Union decided upon at the London summit has been revised. Food and other emergency aid have been provided and trade restrictions eased. However, these factors outlined in the Introduction and Chapter 7 that prevented the G7 from offering any material financial assistance to the Soviet Union did not cease to operate on the day the Moscow coup was defeated or the Commonwealth of Independent States came into existence. As a result, the Gaidar Plan was launched without any effective Western financial assistance and without any certainty as to what kind of assistance would come later. It was, of course, not only the controversial character of this particular plan that was responsible for this uncertainty. Probably also involved were the inherent unpredictability of the post-Soviet situation and the historically rooted theoretical doubt of the possibility of influencing Russia's internal development from the outside. Therefore, Western assistance to Russia and other republics will remain reluctant and delayed, limited, related to certain priority objectives of the Western powers (disarmament), and inadequate in scope and amount to the task of the economic reconstruction of one of the world's largest countries in the foreseeable future.

There is an important message here for Western governments, international financial institutions, commercial banks, and so on, concerning their policies vis-à-vis Central and Eastern Europe. It has to do with the profound differences in political and economic situations and prospects and in the constraints and opportunities for Western policy between the former Soviet Union and Central and Eastern Europe. "Uncertainty" is, of course, a key word for assessing the economic and political future of the Five, but this uncertainty is not to be compared with the unpredictability of future developments in the former Soviet Union. It is not just that Central and East European economies are smaller, closer (in both geographical and other terms) to the West, relatively more developed, and less disrupted than the post-Soviet economy. In addition, these countries can be regarded as established and more or less stable state formations that are governable and offer the scope for relevant economic policies. This means not only that sources of external financing are much easier to establish but also that financial relations with them can in fact influence economic stabilization and political and social development.

All the conclusions of this book concerning the Five's economic relations with the Soviet Union apply to their prospective trade and other relations with Russia and the other republics. To sum up some of the most important points: First, the trade collapse of 1991 is irreversible. The idea of trade stabilization on any level with the successor states of the Soviet Union is illusory. What is more, further reduction in Russian raw-material and energy production, in combination with political problems and difficulties of macroeconomic management, may further weaken the ability of Russia (and the other republics) to deliver goods to the Central and East European countries. Second, despite the decline of 1991, the Soviet Union has remained the Five's most important source of energy imports. Energy (oil, gas, electricity) clearly stands out as a strategic import. The infrastructure for energy imports from other sources is sometimes lacking or insufficient, and, as a consequence of the war in Yugoslavia, the Adriatic pipeline supplying oil to Hungary and Czechoslovakia has been switched off. What this means is that the trade collapse with the Soviet Union (or its successor states) and the Five has not eliminated all of their dangerous dependencies. This remains a task to be accomplished in the coming years. Third, recent domestic developments in the former Soviet Union along with its balance-of-payments crisis make it more obvious than before that collecting outstanding Central and East European claims from the successors of the Soviet Union will be a very difficult (virtually hopeless) task. Last, whereas the tendency of some Western governments, organizations, and banks and of schemes for economic reintegration to approach the former CMEA countries as a group has withstood the end of the Soviet Union, its irrelevance is as clear as ever. Given political change and economic realities, trade stabilization cannot be accomplished by establishing any multilateral payments scheme; whatever the economic theories underlying the various integration schemes, what is essential for the Central and East European countries is discontinuing their dependence on the former Soviet Union and then conducting a strategic reorientation of their economies.

Systemic Transformation: Learning by Doing

It is now apparent how crucial and difficult for the Five's economic survival is management of their relations with both the West and the East. In a more general context, any notion of an impending end to economic decline and ensuing stabilization and improvement in Central and Eastern Europe should be based on drawing some further important conclusions from the mixed experiences of systemic transformation of 1989–1991. This statement pertains to all participants in transformation politics, whether within or outside of Central and Eastern Europe—government authorities, political parties, pressure groups within the region, Western governments, international organizations (from the IMF to the EC), financial institutions, and expert bodies.

Although decisive action is essential to any policy, overconfidence at the outset of the transformation process proved misplaced. Hirschman (1990, p. 20) makes the point:

> Social scientists, historians, and political observers in general agree on one point about the Eastern European revolutions of 1989: no one foresaw them. The collapse of communist power in Eastern Europe, the fall of the Berlin Wall and the reunification of Germany, the implosions in the Soviet Union—the end of the cold war, in short—all these developments unfolded in a remarkably short time and as a huge surprise to "experts" and ordinary television viewers alike. But the lesson—that the utmost modesty is in order when it comes to pronouncements about the future of human societies—does not seem to have sunk in. As soon as those astounding changes in the world's political and economic map took place, numerous voices were heard uttering self-assured opinions about the implications of those changes for this or that country or group of countries. It does not seem to have occurred to

these people that if the events, which are the point of departure for their speculations, were so hard to predict, considerable caution is surely in order when it comes to appraising their impact.

Caution is even more in order when it comes to policy recommendations.[7] The whole process of transformation from a planned to a market economy was until 1989 terra incognita for theory and policy alike. The only effective—controversial but appreciable—experience in demolishing a centrally planned economy was the market-oriented reforms *within* Soviet-type economies prior to 1989, which were explicitly dismissed as unsuccessful and misleading by many architects of transformation schemes. Notwithstanding the history of Western economic development and that of recent liberalization attempts in the developing world, creating a market economy was perceived as a short-term process of "leaping a chasm" rather than a painful long-term task that only begins with the elimination of the Soviet-type system and is based on institution building and continuous organic change of societies and economies in transition. (By "organic" is meant a pattern of development that is based on their own economic and social histories—the recent past, however hideous, included—as well as prevailing conditions, structures, and endogenous developments.) It was frequently considered more important to import the rules and laws of the transition than the capital needed for restructuring. A continuous outflow of resources tended to be considered consistent with the requirements of the transformation process. On largely ideological grounds, any step from plan to market, from centrally directed management of microeconomic activities to liberalization, or from state ownership to private property was considered welcome progress in the right direction. It was overlooked that some of these steps (or their combinations) were poorly engineered, mismanaged, or improperly timed and, as a consequence, were leading to serious deterioration of the macroeconomic situation and sociopolitical strain. Microeconomic differences between market economies and those of Central and Eastern Europe were ignored or underestimated.[8] Lip service to liberalization and privatization was encouraged, and demonstrations of the theoretical difficulties of rapid transition were often declared regressive. Most important, Central and East Europeans were expected to be more Catholic than the Pope, being encouraged to adopt liberalization measures unmatched anywhere except in the textbooks. In a word, it was more or less explicitly suggested that there are certain a priori rules or laws (the equivalent of "general regularities of socialist construction" in Marxist-Leninist parlance) for the creation of a market economy that must be applied in any country moving from a Soviet-type to a market-oriented system.[9]

All this is contradictory to Bairoch's (1988) demonstration that there are no "absolute economic laws," no rules that are valid for every period of history or every economic structure; the same commercial policies (free trade or protectionism) may have various effects in various situations, and what is true for a certain group of countries in a certain historical period may prove false for other countries in other periods.[10]

This highly critical assessment of particular policy actions and policy recommendations may be perceived as biased and exaggerated or as sweeping generalization, but these points must be stressed. The future of Central and Eastern Europe may, to a large extent, depend on the ability and willingness of governments, East and West, and those who advise them to be flexible, pragmatic, and disabused of past fallacies.

Turning from the assessment of the theories and policies of the past two years to the economic outlook for the region, it should be made clear once more that feasible scenarios for the next year or two may range from further (perhaps severe) deterioration of economic situation to maintenance of more or less the present level of production and incomes. The longer-term future may be brighter—depending on what happens in the immediate future—but there is little foundation for any strong predictions. For all practical purposes, within this general framework, the economic performances of different countries may vary as they do today as a function of divergent initial situations, policy decisions, and external environments.

However distressing the short-term forecast may appear, the important point is that even preventing further significant deterioration will require serious policy efforts within and outside the countries concerned and positive changes in Central and Eastern Europe's external conditions. Because of the severe external constraints and the narrowness of the path leading to stabilization and recovery, the importance of pursuing sound domestic policies is tremendous. No general prescriptions can be offered as to what is "sound" and what is not in present-day Central and Eastern Europe. Given the substantial differences between Poland and Romania, or Bulgaria and Czechoslovakia, even the same strategic aims must be pursued by a blend of policies. This does not mean that their similar problems cannot be viewed and analyzed in a common framework.

One such common challenge facing the Five is the necessity of coexisting with and surviving in what they perceive as an environment of relative neglect. Any realistic overview suggests to them that they are not as important to the outside world (which in their present *Weltanschauung* is the Western world) as they would hope. They have some weighty arguments for persuading outsiders to reconsider this attitude, and it is imperative that they not give up the struggle for a rethinking of Western policy. Yet they should not harbor any illusions of an imminent change in that policy or its capacity to free them of the pain of devising and implementing stable domestic policies of economic transformation. In fact, under *any* Western policy, most of the burden of transformation will be borne by the societies themselves, and almost all of the management must be done by the governments of the countries involved.

Neglect on the part of the outside world is, of course, a relative matter. It is only in comparison with early promises and with their own expectations and perceived economic and social needs that the Five are not receiving the necessary financial and economic attention. By any other criterion, Central and Eastern Europe is the focus of international attention, and other regions of the world are afraid of being neglected as the world turns to the former East. More important, as is emphasized by Hirschman, neglect is not all bad. The history of the past two years suggests that it is dangerous when overemphasis in political and ideological terms and relative neglect in financial terms coincide. Although money for Central and Eastern Europe has been scarce, outside attitudes toward the transformation process have been shaped more by considerations of international policy and theory than by the hard and varied economic realities of the region. This duality may be in part responsible for the misconceptions and mistakes of these years. A more pragmatic, modest approach may emerge from a recognition by the governments concerned of the implications of relative neglect. Only concentrating on how to brake economic decline and prevent disorganization and disintegration of their economies can lead to meaningful systemic transformation.

Notwithstanding the tremendous difficulties examined in this book, it is sensible to conclude it on an optimistic note. The future of the economies and societies in Central and Eastern Europe is very unclear. The political changes of 1989 and 1990 have, however, brought not only uncertainty but a certain confidence. As a matter of fact, until the very last months of ancien régime, Central and East Europeans cherished no illusions that the economic and political system they had been living under was approaching an end. Even amidst multiple signs of decline, neither critics nor opponents questioned the inevitability of the old system's surviving for decades or even centuries. No one was able to put forth any viable alternative to that historical cul-de-sac. (This is why alternatives were sought within the system, that is, systemic reform.) In this respect, the changes in Central and Eastern Europe are most profound. The inevitability of long-term historical impasse, of remaining on the periphery of global development, is no longer assumed. Given such a difficult legacy, transformation will of necessity be a protracted process. The theoretical possibility of opening up to and catching up with the developed world has, however, been established. If Central and Eastern Europe miss this chance, it is the current policies of those involved in this region's economic and political development that will have to be blamed.

Notes

1. Compliance with the targets agreed on with the IMF in itself is no insurance that debt can be managed. For example, matured debts must be refinanced by fresh ones—a difficult undertaking given the commercial banks' withdrawal from the region. But the important point is that in the most cases agreements with the IMF make external financing theoretically feasible.

2. What follows draws extensively on Köves and Oblath (1991).

3. "Debt relief" is understood as actions agreed upon by the creditor(s) and the debtor, explicit or implied, that reduce the sum of the debt repayment and/or postpone it, sometimes also easing the fulfillment of the debt repayment with additional loans.

4. According to preliminary trade data based on customs statistics, hard-currency exports increased by 40 percent and totaled $10.2 billion in 1991. Imports increased by about 85 percent and totaled $11.7 billion. This amounts to a deficit of about $1.5 billion. The important point is that a considerable proportion of the commodities imported has been foreign direct investment in kind. Therefore, the trade deficit on the current account has been more modest.

5. The overwhelming majority of Hungarian debt is owed to commercial banks of three countries: Austria, Germany, and Japan. Therefore, the proposal involves the financing of interest owed to commercial banks with government funds of the respective countries. Another possibility for banks interested in the Hungarian modernization fund is the use of interest from the fund to finance investment in Hungary. The fund would be managed by the governmental authorities of the creditor countries and/or interested banks and could be used to finance investment in infrastructure and privatization (purchasing shares of Hungarian state-owned companies).

6. Perhaps one should not go that far. The example of the Romanian debt repayment policies in the 1980s provides the clearest idea of how high the price is, in terms of overall economic and social decline and political repression, of forced debt management. In practical terms, the Romanian case is an extreme one. No one is asking Hungary to repay all its outstanding debt in a short period of time. Nevertheless, the message is unmistakable: "successful" debt management that disregards costs and risks may lead to the very same place as default.

7. David Stark (1990, p. 353) also makes this point: "For all too many Western observers, the severity of the economic crises in the countries of East Central Europe appears as an open invitation to offer policy prescriptions for measures to bring about the full marketization of those economies. At the same time, the dramatic changes being proposed elicit equally well-meaning advice from other Western observers who, with an equal dose of paternalism, urge caution on Polish and Hungarian policy makers perceived to hold naive views about 'the market.' "

8. For a stimulating discussion on this point see Vanous (1991) and Hinds (1991).

9. Interestingly, the most successful recent examples of catching up with the developed world by Japan and the countries of Southeast Asia were more or less ignored in devising reform scenarios for Central and Eastern Europe. To be sure, Far Eastern economic and social conditions and experiences are unique in many ways. What is more, liberalization and (in some countries) privatization in those countries were on the governments' agendas but not as part of "systemic transition." A further important point is that forty years of experience of government mismanagement of the economy and mistaken, inward-oriented industrial policies in the framework of the CMEA have produced a more or less general skepticism among Central and East Europeans with regard to the feasibility of any successful economic planning and industrial (sectoral) policies in *their* countries. Notwithstanding these and other specifics, Far Eastern experiences concerning, for example, the interrelationships of regulation and liberalization or consensus building between government, business, and unions would be of some relevance in Central and Eastern Europe (Yoshitomi 1991).

10. Bairoch suggests that "to a very large extent past experience of more developed countries can be beneficial for today's less developed countries," but the economists' "task is a very difficult one since they have to find cures for many rapidly mutating patients" (1988, p. 21).

Bibliography

Abdulai, Seyyid. "The Opening of the East and Its Implications for the South." *West-Ost-Journal* (Vienna) no. 6, December 1990.

Aslund, Anders. "Principles of Privatization." In Csaba, L. (ed.), *Systemic Change and Stabilization in Eastern Europe*. Aldershot: Dartmouth, 1991, pp. 17–31.

Bairoch, Paul. "The Paradoxes of Economic History: Economic Laws and History." Alfred Marshall Lecture, European Economic Association, Third Annual Congress, Bologna, Italy, 27–29 August 1988.

Balázs, Páeter. "New Ways of Enlarging the European Integration to East European Countries: The Case of Hungary." Paper presented at the conference "Impediments to Transition: The East European Countries and the Policies of the European Community," Florence, Italy, 24–25 January 1992.

Begg, David. "Economic Reform in Czechoslovakia: Should We Believe in Santa Klaus?" Paper presented at "Economic Policy: A European Forum," Thirteenth Panel Meeting, 18–19 April 1991.

Berend, Iván T. "Uj Marshall-tervre lenne szükség" (A new Marshall Plan would be necessary). *Népszabadság* (Budapest),11 January 1991.

Blommestein, H., and Marrese, M. (eds.): *Transformation of Planned Economies: Property Rights Reform and Macroeconomic Stability*. Paris: OECD, 1991.

Blommestein, H., Marrese, M., and Zecchini, S. "Centrally Planned Economies in Transition: An Introductory Overview of Selected Issues and Strategies." In Bloomestein H., and Marrese, M. (eds.), *Transformation of Planned Economies: Property Rights Reform and Macroeconomic Stability*. Paris: OECD, 1991, pp. 11–28.

Blue Ribbon Commission. *Hungary in Transformation to Freedom and Prosperity*. Indianapolis: Hudson Institute, 1991.

Brainard, Lawrence. "Strategies for Economic Transformation in Eastern Europe: The Role of Financial Reform." In Blommestein H., and Marrese, M. (eds.), *Transformation of Planned Economies: Property Rights Reform and Macroeconomic Stability*. Paris: OECD, 1991, pp. 95–108.

Brzezinski, Zbigniew. "For Eastern Europe, a $25 Billion Aid Package." *New York Times*, 7 March 1990.

Collins, Susan, and Rodrik, Dani. *Eastern Europe and the Soviet Union in the World Economy*. Washington, D.C.: Institute for International Economics, 1991.

Csaba, László. "Between Comecon and the Market." Unpublished manuscript, 1991(a).

———. "Is Regional Cooperation the Key?" *Transition* 2, no. 3, 1991(b).

Czinkota, Michael. "The EC '92 and Eastern Europe: Effects of Integration vs. Disintegration." *Columbia Journal of World Business* 26, no. 2, Spring 1991, pp. 20–27.

Dhanji, Farid, and Milanovic, Branko. "Privatization." In Marer, Paul, and Zecchini,

Salvatore (eds.), *The Transition to a Market Economy in Central and Eastern Europe*. Vol. 2, *Special Issues*. Paris: OECD, 1991.
Dornbusch, Rudi. "Strategies and Priorities for Reform." In Marer, Paul, and Zecchini, Salvatore (eds.), *The Transition to a Market Economy in Central and Eastern Europe*. Vol. 1, *The Broad Issues*. Paris: OECD, 1991.
ECE (Economic Commission for Europe). *Economic Survey of Europe 1989-1990*. New York: United Nations, 1990.
———. *Economic Bulletin for Europe*. Vol. 42/90. New York: United Nations, 1991(a).
———. *Economic Survey of Europe in 1990-1991*. New York: United Nations, 1991(b).
Eichengreen, Barry, and Portes, Richard. "Dealing with Debt: The 1930's and the 1980's." In Husain, Ishrat, and Diwan, Ishac (eds.), *Dealing with the Debt Crisis*. Washington, D.C.: World Bank, 1989, pp. 69-86.
ETLA (The Research Institute of the Finnish Economy). *The Finnish Economy*. No. 1, 1991.
Fischer, Stanley. "Privatization in East European Transformation." Paper presented at the conference "The Transition to a Market Economy: Institutional Aspects," Prague, Czechoslovakia, 24-27 March 1991.
Fischer, Stanley, and Gelb, Alan. "Issues in Socialist Economy Reform." In Marer, Paul, and Zecchini, Salvatore (eds.), *The Transition to a Market Economy in Central and Eastern Europe*. Vol. 1, *The Broad Issues*. OECD, 1991.
Gács, János. "Foreign Trade Liberalization (1968-1990)." In Köves, András, and Marer, Paul (eds.), *Foreign Economic Liberalization: Transformations in Socialist and Market Economies*. Boulder: Westview Press, 1991.
Gaidar, Yegor. "Russia Needs Three Kinds of Economic Aid—and Quickly." *Financial Times*, 22 January 1992.
Hinds, Manuel. "Comment on Jan Vanous' Article." *Transition*, 2, no. 6, June 1991.
Hirschman, Albert O. "Good News Is Not Bad News." *New York Review of Books*, 10 October 1990.
Hormats, Robert M. "As Comecon Fades, the East Needs a Hand." *International Herald Tribune*, 21 November 1989.
Horváth, D. Tamás. "A privatizáció buktatói Kelet-Európában" (Dilemmas of Privatization in Eastern Europe). *Külgazdaság* (Budapest), August 1991, pp. 16-26.
Hrnčíř, Miroslav. "Transition to a Market-Type Economy: The Case of Czechoslovakia." *Most* (Bologna), no. 2, 1991, pp. 21-32.
Husain, Ishrat, and Diwan, Ishac. "External Debt and Expected Net Flows." In Marer, Paul, and Zecchini, Salvatore (eds.), *The Transition to a Market Economy in Central and Eastern Europe*. Vol. 2, *Special Issues*. Paris: OECD, 1991.
Inotai, András. "Liberalization and Foreign Direct Investment." In Köves, András, and Marer, Paul (eds.), *Foreign Economic Liberalization: Transformations in Socialist and Market Economies*. Boulder: Westview Press, 1991.
Inotai, András, and Patai, Mihály. "Adósságkezelési stratégia a kilencvenes évekre" (A Hungarian debt management strategy for the 1990s). Unpublished manuscript, May 1991.
Katz, Stanley. "East Europe Should Learn from Asia." *Financial Times*, 24 April 1991.
Kenen, Peter. "Transitional Arrangements for Trade and Payments Among the CMEA Countries." *IMF Staff Papers* 38, no 2, June 1991, pp. 235-266.

Kolodko, Grzegorz W. "Polish Hyperinflation and Stabilization 1989-1990." *Most* (Bologna), no. 1, 1991, pp. 9-36.
Komarek, Valtr. "Economic Shock Therapy Endangers the Patients." *International Herald Tribune*, 7 January 1992.
KOPINT-DATORG (Institute for Economic and Market Research and Informatics, Budapest). "Economic Trends in Hungary, Eastern Europe and the World Economy." Autumn 1990.

———. "Economic Trends in Eastern Europe and the World Economy." Spring 1991(a).

———. "A müködötöke befogadása és szabályozása: nemzetközi és hazai tapasztalatok" (Hosting and regulation of foreign direct investment: International and Hungarian experiences). Unpublished manuscript, Budapest, 1991(b).

Kornai, János. *The Economics of Shortage*. Amsterdam: North Holland, 1980.

———. "The Hungarian Reform Process: Visions, Hopes, and Reality." *Journal of Economic Literature* 24, no. 4, December 1986, pp. 1687-1737.

———. *The Road to a Free Economy: Shifting from a Socialist System, the Example of Hungary*. New York: Norton, 1990(a).

———. "The Affinity between Ownership and Coordination Mechanisms: The Common Experience of Reform in Socialist Countries." Helsinki: World Institute for Development Economics Research, 1990(b).

Kostrzewa, Wojciech, Nunnenkamp, Peter, and Schmieding, Holger. "A Marshall Plan for Middle and Eastern Europe?" *The World Economy* 13, no. 1, March 1990, pp. 27-50.

Kostrzewa, Wojciech, and Schmieding, Holger. "EFTA Option for the Reform States of Eastern Europe." *The World Economy* 12, no. 4, December 1989.

Köves, András. "'Implicit Subsidies' and Some Issues of Economic Relations Within the CMEA." *Acta Oeconomica* (Budapest) 31, nos. 1-2, 1983, pp. 125-136.

———. *The CMEA Countries in the World Economy: Turning Inwards or Turning Outwards*. Budapest: Akadémiai, 1985.

———. "A New Situation in Hungarian-Soviet Trade: What Is To Be Done?" In Marrese, Michael, and Richter, Sándor (eds.), *The Challenge of Simultaneous Economic Relations with East and West*. London: Macmillan, 1990, pp. 64-79.

———. "Transforming Commercial Relations within the CMEA: The Case of Hungary." In Köves, András, and Marer, Paul (eds.), *Foreign Economic Liberalization: Transformations in Socialist and Market Economies*. Boulder: Westview Press, 1991, pp. 171-185.

Köves, András, and Marer, Paul (eds.). *Foreign Economic Liberalization: Transformations in Socialist and Market Economies*. Boulder: Westview Press, 1991(a).

———. "Economic Liberalization in Eastern Europe and in Market Economies." In Köves, András, and Marer, Paul (eds.), *Foreign Economic Liberalization: Transformations in Socialist and Market Economies*. Boulder: Westview Press, 1991(b), pp. 15-33.

Köves, András, and Oblath, Gábor. "Stabilization and Foreign Economic Policy in Hungary." *Acta Oeconomica* 43, nos. 1-2, 1991, pp. 1-18.

Langhammer, Rolf. "Liberalization Attempts and Outcomes." In Köves, András, and Marer, Paul (eds.), *Foreign Economic Liberalization: Transformations in Socialist and Market Economies*. Boulder: Westview Press, 1991(a), pp. 57-70.

———. "Competition Among Developing Countries for Foreign Investment in the Eighties—Whom Did OECD Investors Prefer?" *Weltwirtschaftliches Archiv* 127, no. 2, 1991(b), pp. 390–403.

Levcik, Friedrich. "The Case for a Gradualist Approach to Convertibility." Paper presented at the conference on East European convertibility, Vienna, Austria, 20–22 January 1991.

Lipton, David, and Sachs, Jeffrey. "Privatization in Eastern Europe: The Case of Poland." Paper presented at the conference "Adjustment and Growth: Lessons for Eastern Europe," Pultusk, Poland, 4–5 October 1990(a).

———. "Creating a Market Economy in Eastern Europe: The Case of Poland." *Brookings Papers on Economic Activity*, no. 1, 1990(b).

Lóránt, Károly. "Liberalizmusra ítélve" (Sentenced to liberalism). *Magyar Nemzet* (Budapest), 17 November 1990.

Marer, Paul, and Zecchini, Salvatore (eds.). *The Transition to a Market Economy in Central and Eastern Europe.* Vol. 1, *The Broad Issues;* Vol. 2, *Special Isues.* Paris: OECD, 1991.

Marrese, Michael, and Richter, Sándor (eds.). *The Challenge of Simultaneous Economic Relations with East and West.* London: Macmillan, 1990.

Marrese, Michael, and Vanous, Jan. *Soviet Subsidization of Trade with Eastern Europe: A Soviet Perspective.* Berkeley: University of California Institute of International Studies, 1983.

Mihályi, Péter, and Smolik, Joseph. "Lending Is Not Enough: An Assessment of Western Support for Reform in Hungary and Poland, 1989–1990." *Communist Economies and Economic Transformation* 3, no. 2, 1991, pp. 201–220.

Moisi, Dominique, and Rupnik, Jacques. "Making Eastern Europe Work Is the West's Problem." *International Herald Tribune*, 12 April 1991.

Móra, Mária. "Changes in the Structure and Ownership Form of State Enterprises (1987–1990)." *Economic Research Institute Economic Papers* (Budapest), 1990, pp. 5–22.

Musatov, Valery. "'Taifun'—peremen" (The "typhoon" of changes). *Pravda*, 13 March 1991.

Norman, Peter. "Glass Houses in the G7." *Financial Times*, 20–21 July 1991.

Nuti, Mario. "Privatization in Socialist Economies: General Issues and the Polish Case." In Blommestein, H., and Marrese, M. (eds.), *Transformation of Planned Economies: Property Rights Reform and Macroeconomic Stability.* Paris: OECD, 1991, pp. 51–64.

Oblath, Gábor. "Internal Regulation of Foreign Trade with Respect to Socialist Trading Partners: A Comparison of the Finnish and the Hungarian Systems." In Marrese, Michael, and Richter, Sándor (eds.), *The Challenge of Simultaneous Economic Relations with East and West.* London: Macmillan, 1990, pp. 109–125.

———. "Trade Policy Recommendations." In Köves, András, and Marer, Paul (eds.), *Foreign Economic Liberalization: Transformations in Socialist and Market Economies.* Boulder: Westview Press, 1991(a), pp. 207–218.

———. Discussion of papers by L. Bokros and J. Zahradnik, prepared for the conference on East European convertibility, Vienna, Austria, 20–22 January 1991(b).

———. "Instant Convertibility or Gradual Liberalization?" *The Hungarian Economy* 19, no. 3, 1991(c).

OECD. *Economic Outlook.* No. 49. Paris: OECD, July 1991(a).

―――. *Financial Market Trends.* Paris: OECD, February 1991(b).
―――. *OECD Economic Surveys: Hungary 1991.* Paris: OECD 1991(c).
―――. *Economic Outlook.* No. 50. Paris: OECD, December 1991(d).
Petschnig, Mária Zita, and Voszka, Éva. "Tulajdonosi szerkezetváltás—Infláció" (Restructuring ownership and inflation). Unpublished manuscript, Financial Research, Inc., Budapest, 1991.
Pick, Milos. "Quo vadis—homo sapiens? (The Results and Alternatives of the Transformation Strategy of the CSFR)." Unpublished manuscript, 1991.
Portes, Richard. "The European Community and Eastern Europe After 1992." In Padoa-Schioppa, Tommaso (ed.), *Europe After 1992: Three Essays.* Princeton University Essays in International Finance, no. 182, May 1991.
Research Institute for Foreign Economic Relations. *ČSFR in International Economy Quarterly.* June 1991.
Richter, Sándor. "Is There a Future for Regional Economic Cooperation in Eastern Europe?" Paper presented at the conference "Whither Socialist Society: Economic and Political Transition in the Soviet Union and Eastern Europe," Jerusalem, Israel, 8–13 April 1991.
Rohatyn, Felix G. "Monnet, Not Mao Had the Vision the East Needs Now." *International Herald Tribune,* 21 November 1989.
Rosati, Dariusz. "The Sequencing of Reforms and Policy Measures in the Transition from Central Planning to Market: The Polish Experience." Paper presented at the conference "The Transition to a Market Economy in Central and Eastern Europe," Paris, France, 28–30 November 1990.
―――. "Sequencing the Reforms in Poland." In Marer, Paul, and Zecchini, Salvatore (eds.), *The Transition to a Market Economy in Central and Eastern Europe.* Vol. 1, *The Broad Issues.* Paris: OECD, 1991.
Sachs, Jeffrey. "Conditionality, Debt Relief, and the Developing Country Debt Crisis." In Sachs, Jeffrey (ed.), *Developing Country Debt and the World Economy.* Chicago: University of Chicago Press, 1989.
―――. "Poland and Eastern Europe: What Is to Be Done?" In Köves, András, and Marer, Paul (eds.), *Foreign Economic Liberalization: Transformations in Socialist and Market Economies.* Boulder: Westview Press, 1991(a), pp. 235–246.
―――. "Privatization Is Top Priority in Eastern Europe, Says Sachs." *IMF Survey,* 27 May 1991(b).
―――. "Goodwill Is Not Enough." *The Economist,* 3 January 1992.
Stark, David. "Privatization in Hungary: From Plan to Market or From Plan to Clan?" *East European Politics and Societies* 4, no. 3, Fall 1990, pp. 351–392.
―――. "Privatization in East Central Europe." *Cornell University Center for International Studies Working Papers on Transition from State Socialism,* no. 6. 1991.
Szabó-Szuba, Jolanta, "Poland's Hard Currency Debt." Unpublished manuscript, KOPINT-DATORG, Budapest: 1991.
Tardos, Márton. "Economic Organizations and Ownership." *Acta Oeconomica* 40, nos. 1–2, 1989, pp. 17–37.
―――. "Liberalization and Privatization." In Köves, András, and Marer, Paul (eds.), *Foreign Economic Liberalization: Transformations in Socialist and Market Economies.* Boulder: Westview Press, 1991, pp. 255–260.

UN Statistical Office, International Monetary Fund, and International Bank for Reconstruction and Development. *Direction of International Trade: Annual Data for the Years 1937, 1938, and 1948–1952*. Statistical Papers Series T, 4, nos. 1–2, 1953.

Vanous, Jan. "Nuts and Bolts of Economic Reform in Central and Eastern Europe." *Transition* 2, no. 6, June 1991.

Williamson, John. *The Economic Opening of Eastern Europe*. Washington, D.C.: Institute for International Economics, 1991.

Yoshitomi, Masaru. "Selected Country Studies: Japan." In Marer, Paul, and Zecchini, Salvatore (eds.), *The Transition to a Market Economy in Central and Eastern Europe*. Vol 1, *The Broad Issues*. Paris: OECD, 1991.

About the Book
and Author

In this volume, a leading Hungarian economist considers the wide range of experiences that Central and East European countries have had during their first two years of economic reform. András Köves pinpoints key differences within the region as well as identifying common themes—including economic decline, mounting social tension, and political strife.

Within this context, Köves addresses the basic problems of transformation, offering a comparative analysis of the various approaches to economic stabilization and liberalization—"shock therapy" versus a more gradual change—as well as exploring the dilemmas of privatization. Because of the complexity of the issues involved in economic transformation, he argues that the mainstream approach that advocates speed as the most important factor of change is misleading.

The book focuses especially on foreign economic policies that—in light of the unprecedented isolationism created by the CMEA—are of particular importance for the delicate transformation process. Köves analyzes the factors that have contributed to the collapse of trade with the former Soviet Union while creating obstacles to economic integration in postcommunist Central and Eastern Europe. He contends that "joining Europe" and being integrated into the international economy are pivotal for stabilization and transformation but that inherent structural weaknesses and enormous foreign debt will make economic reorientation an extremely difficult undertaking. Responsibility will inevitably fall to the West to create an external environment conducive to internal transition, and Köves contends that in view of recent political developments in and around the region, Western stakes in its political and economic stabilization are much higher than generally believed.

András Köves is deputy general director of research, Institute for Economic and Market Research and Informatics, Budapest, Hungary.

Index

Agriculture, 96, 97–98, 102(n9)
Aid
    and dollar-accounted trade, 60, 65
    and EC association agreements, 97
    intraregional cooperation conditions for, 90–91
    to Poland, 21, 103, 104–106
    Soviet, to East bloc, 65–66. *See also* Subsidies, Soviet "implicit"
    to Soviet Union, 72, 114, 125–126
    stability concerns and Western, 12–14, 113–115, 122–124, 126
    Western policy on, 103–113, 115(n1), 116(n8), 117(nn 10, 11, 12), 125–126, 129–130
Albania, 7, 14(n1), 102(n5)
Andriessen, Frans, 100
Asia, 57(n8), 118(n13). *See also* Southeast Asia
Asian Development Bank, 118(n13)
Aslund, Anders, 37
Association agreements, 95–100, 102(nn 4, 5). *See also* Free trade agreements
Austerity measures
    Bulgarian, 25, 116(n4)
    Czechoslovakian, 31
    and debt management, 19, 109, 111
    Polish, 24
    and transition, 21, 27, 119, 121
Austria, 77(n10)
Autarky, 49–50
Authoritarianism, 115

Bairoch, Paul, 128, 131(n10)
Balcerowicz, Leszek, 14(n3), 20, 24
Balcerowicz Plan, 104, 125

Baltic states, 102(n5)
Bank for International Settlements, 92(n3)
Banks
    and Central and East European credit worthiness, 104–108, 107(table), 116(nn 6, 7)
    and debt forgiveness, 110
    and government policy, 111
    and investment of interest payments, 131(n5)
Bashkiria, 11
Bogomolov, Oleg, 75(n5)
Brussels Commission, 97, 98
Bulgaria
    and CMEA trade, 60, 65, 67
    and commodity shortages, 19
    debt management, 106, 116(nn 4, 6)
    economic decline in, 2, 120
    and European integration, 95, 102(n5)
    and foreign investment, 54, 57(nn 1, 10)
    political factors in, 20, 115
    transition policy in, 25, 34(n1)
    and Western aid policy, 109

CAP. *See* Common Agricultural Policy
Capital. *See* Investment
Centralization
    and CMEA trade, 63, 64, 73
    and privatization, 42, 48(n14)
    and Soviet transition process, 125
China, 7
CMEA. *See* Council for Mutual Economic Assistance
Cocom. *See* Coordinating Committee

141

Commercialization, 38–39
Common Agricultural Policy (CAP), 98, 102(n10)
Common Market, 92(n5)
Commonwealth of Independent States
  and economic transition, 124
  instability within, 11, 13, 74, 82
  See also Soviet Union
Communication, 55
Compensation. *See* Restitution
Convertibility
  and Czechoslovakia, 31
  and East Germany, 28–29
  and Hungary, 57(n4)
  Polish program, 21, 22, 23–24
  and Russian transition policy, 125
  and transition policy, 25–27, 119
  See also Currency; Trade
Coordinating Committee (Cocom), 103
Council for Mutual Economic Assistance (CMEA), 14(n1)
  change in currency of trade, 63–71
  collapse of, 9, 59–61, 61(table), 70–71, 77(n15), 79–80
  cooperative projects, 8, 76(n8)
  economic relations within, 7, 49, 62–63, 76(n9), 77(nn 12, 13, 14), 80
  Hungarian reforms, 75(nn 3, 5)
Credit
  extending, to Soviet Union, 71–72
  Soviet letters of, 70
  and Western attitudes, 121
  worthiness and commercial banks, 106–108
  See also Debt
Csaba, László, 73
Cuba, 14(n1)
Currency
  CMEA trade, 59, 63–71, 75(n5), 76(n6). *See also* Council for Mutual Economic Assistance
  consumer confidence in, 19
  devaluation, 21, 22, 23–24, 31, 35(n12), 102(n12), 119
  German revaluation of, 28–29, 35(nn 16, 17)
  See also Convertibility
Customs. *See* Tariffs
Czechoslovakia
  and Central and East European cooperation, 84
  and CMEA trade, 60, 66, 67, 76(n7), 79
  credit worthiness of, 106–108, 116(n6), 123
  economic decline in, 2, 15(n8), 120
  and European integration, 52, 95, 98
  and foreign investment, 53, 54, 57(nn 1, 10)
  political destabilization potential, 115
  privatization in, 44–45, 47(n5), 48(n14), 57(n9)
  socialist legacy in, 3, 7
  transition policy in, 26, 30–32, 34(n1)

Deák, János, 75(n5)
Debt
  and East Germany, 28
  enterprise, 39
  forgiveness for Poland, 23, 104–106, 116(n3), 122
  and Hungary, 33, 104, 116(n2), 120–124, 131(n5)
  management, 120–124, 130(nn 1, 3), 131(n6)
  management and foreign investment, 52, 57(n8)
  relation to economic crisis of, 4–6, 15(nn 8, 10), 19, 50, 84, 104, 105(table), 106(table), 107(table), 116(n6)
  Soviet, 70, 124
  and trade with Soviets, 8, 76(n8)
  and Western aid policy, 103–109
Decentralization, 42. *See also* Centralization
Demand
  cutting domestic, 22, 27, 119

for state-owned property, 42–43
  See also Shortage economy
Democracy
  and credit issues, 116(n7)
  and joining Europe, 11, 93, 100
  See also Political change
Devaluation
  and cutting domestic demand, 119
  and Czechoslovakia, 31
  and EC trade, 102(n12)
  of Polish currency, 21, 22, 23–24, 35(n12)
Developing countries, 110, 117(n11)
Development
  and European integration, 94
  and Far East, 131(n9)
  and incurring debt, 5
  reducing debt service to finance, 123, 131(n5)
  Soviet legacy of, 7, 62
  See also Economic transition; Integration
Dornbusch, Rudi, 18, 34(n4)

East European Payments Union (EEPU), 81, 82–83, 92(n3), 116(n8)
EBRD. *See* European Bank for Reconstruction and Development
EC. *See* European Community
Economic decline
  and collapse of CMEA trade, 6–9, 60, 64, 84. *See also* Council for Mutual Economic Assistance
  and foreign investment, 52
  and indebtedness, 4, 5–6, 104. *See also* Debt
  and integration schemes, 89–90
  during 1980s, 3–4, 19–20
  and privatization, 43. *See also* Privatization
  of Soviet Union, 6, 10, 60–61, 72–74, 82

and transition process, 1–2, 31, 33–34, 34(n4), 46, 109, 119–120, 130
  See also Stabilization
Economic systems, 17, 34(nn 1, 2)
Economic transition
  and CMEA dollar-accounted trade, 59–71, 75(nn 1, 4, 5), 76(nn 7, 8)
  current status and future of, 119–120, 127–130
  and Czechoslovakia, 30–32
  difficulties of, 1–2, 14, 34(n4)
  East German, 27–30
  and EC inclusion, 93–94, 100–101
  and former Soviet Union, 124–126
  gradual versus rapid, 17–34, 34(n3).
    See also Gradualism; Shock therapy
  and Hungary, 32–34
  Polish program for, 20–25
  privatization and investment issues, 37–46, 52–56. *See also* Privatization
  trade liberalization and reorientation, 50–52, 71–75, 79–92, 126–127.
    See also Integration
  and Western aid policy, 103, 108–115, 122–124, 125–126, 129–130
  Yugoslavian program, 26
  See also Liberalization; Policy; Stabilization
Economist, 37, 44
Education, 4
EEPU. *See* East European Payments Union
EFTA. *See* European Free Trade Association
Energy, 7, 8, 59–60, 67–68, 68(table), 126–127
Environment, 4, 31
Ethnic conflict, 12, 115. *See also* Stability
European Bank for Reconstruction and Development (EBRD), 116(n8)
European Community (EC)
  aid from, 72

association agreements, 89, 95–100, 102(nn 4, 5)
Central and Eastern European integration into, 52, 83, 93–95, 100–101
membership and intra–Central European relations, 91
and stability concerns, 12. *See also* Stability
See also West
European Economic Area, 97
European Free Trade Association (EFTA), 52, 89, 97, 101(n1)
Exchange rates, 15(n10). *See also* Convertibility
Exports
collapse of CMEA, 60, 68–71, 72–73
geographical distributions of, 86(Table 5.1), 87(table)
and Hungary, 121
and international competitiveness, 98
liberalizing, 51
See also Trade

Financial regulations, 96, 99. *See also* Legal issues
Financing. *See* Credit
Finland, 77(n10)
Fischer, Stanley, 1, 40
Foreign economic relations
among Central European countries, 80–92
and CMEA trading bloc, 59–75, 80. *See also* Council for Mutual Economic Assistance
and debt management, 120–124. *See also* Debt
and the EC, 93–101. *See also* European Community
and foreign direct investment, 52–56. *See also* Investment
role in transition of, 27, 49–50, 56
trade liberalization, 18, 50–52
and Western aid, 103–115. *See also* Aid

See also Integration; International economy; Trade
France, 98, 102(n9)
Free trade agreements, 101(n1)

Gaidar Plan, 13, 125, 126
GATT. *See* General Agreement on Tariffs and Trade
GDP. *See* Gross domestic product
GDR. *See* German Democratic Republic
Gelb, Alan, 1
General Agreement on Tariffs and Trade (GATT), 51
German Democratic Republic (GDR)
and CMEA trade, 59
debt in, 116(n6)
investment in, 53
privatization in, 42
transition and reunification, 14(n1), 27–30, 35(nn 16, 17), 36(n18). *See also* Germany
German Economic and Monetary Union, 59
Germany
and aid, 110
reunification, 10, 28–30, 59
trade with, 100(n3)
See also German Democratic Republic
Gorbachev, Mikhail, 114, 118(n14)
Government expenditures, 21, 121. *See also* Debt; Subsidies
Gradualism
and convertibility, 27
and Czechoslovakia, 30–32
and debt management, 123
and Hungary, 32–34, 36(n19)
and Polish transition program, 20
versus rapid change, 30
See also Economic transition; Shock therapy
Gross domestic product (GDP)
and Czechoslovakia, 31
and Poland, 24

Index   145

transition and decreases in, 2
  See also Economic decline
G7 economic summit (1989), 103
Gulf war, 59–60

Health, 4
Hirschman, Albert, 117(n11), 127–128
Hormats, Robert, 108
Horváth, D. Tamás, 38
Hungarian National Bank. *See* National Bank of Hungary
Hungarian-Soviet Committee of Economists, 66
Hungary
  and Central and East European cooperation, 84
  and CMEA trade, 60, 63, 65–67, 75(nn 2, 3, 5), 76(n7)
  debt and credit issues in, 104, 106–108, 116(nn 2, 6), 120–124, 131(nn 4, 5)
  economic decline in, 2, 15(n7), 19, 111, 120
  and European integration, 52, 95, 96–97, 98, 99
  and foreign investment, 53, 54, 55, 56, 57(nn 1, 10)
  living standards in, 14(n5)
  opening to West of, 6, 9, 15(n9), 32–33
  political destabilization potential, 20, 114–115
  privatization in, 42, 47(nn 5, 7, 9, 11, 12), 54
  socialist legacy, 3, 7
  trade liberalization policy, 51, 57(nn 3, 4)
  transition policy in, 32–34, 34(n1), 35(n6), 36(n19)
  and Western aid policy, 103, 109

IMF. *See* International Monetary Fund
Imports
  energy, 60, 67–68, 68(table), 126–127

  geographical distributions of, 86(Table 5.2), 88(table)
  liberalization policies, 51, 57(n3)
  to Soviet Union, 77(nn 10, 11)
Income. *See* Wages
Inflation, 23(Table 1.1)
  in Czechoslovakia, 31
  and former Soviet Union, 125
  in Hungary, 19, 33
  in Poland, 19, 22, 24, 25, 35(n10)
  and transition process, 2, 37, 119
  in Yugoslavia, 26
Infrastructure
  and importing oil, 67, 126–127
  regional destruction of, 4
Instability. *See* Stability
Integration
  within Central and Eastern Europe, 80–92, 92(n4)
  and European Community, 93–101
  and foreign investment, 52, 53
  and Soviet Union, 10–11, 91–92, 92(n2)
  See also Trade
Interest rates, 6
International Bank for Economic Cooperation, 76(n8)
International economy
  economic transformation and, 50, 93–94. *See also* Economic transition
  indebtedness and opening to, 5–6, 15(n9). *See also* Debt
  politics and opening to, 11. *See also* Political change
  See also Foreign economic relations; Integration; Trade; West
International Investment Bank, 76(n8)
International Monetary Fund (IMF)
  and conditional assistance agreements, 109–111
  and debt management, 120, 121, 130(n1)
  and Hungary, 15(n9)
  and Poland, 20, 104
  and Romania, 117(n9)

and Soviet Union, 118(n15)
and transition to dollar-accounted
  trade, 65
and Yugoslavia, 26
Investment
  and debt crisis, 57(n8)
  and development financing, 131(n5)
  domestic ambivalence about foreign,
    44
  and East Germany, 29
  and EC membership, 99
  and global capital shortage, 109–110
  and Hungary, 121
  laws on foreign, 41
  motivations for foreign, 58(n11), 103
  Polish volumes, 24
  and private sector development, 40,
    43, 57(nn 6, 10)
  and privatization, 38, 39, 44–45,
    47(n9), 53, 54–56, 57(n9)
  role in transition of foreign, 5, 49,
    52–56, 57(n7)
  and socialist governments, 50, 57(n1)
  in Soviet energy projects, 8
  See also Credit; Resources

Japan, 77(n14), 94, 131(n9)
Joint ventures, 8, 55–56, 57(nn 1, 10)

Klaus, Vaclav, 79
Kornai, János, 38, 46(n2)

Lamont, Norman, 102(n10)
Latin America, 57(n8), 108–109
Legal issues
  and European integration, 96, 99,
    102(n6)
  and privatization, 41–42
  See also Policy
Levcik, Friedrich, 22–23
Liberalization
  and convertibility, 26–27. *See also*
    Convertibility
  and EC membership conditions, 97,
    99, 102(n10)

and foreign investment, 49
gradual versus rapid, 21–22, 30
and Polish program, 21
role in transition of, 18–19, 128
and Russia, 125
and socialist governments, 35(n6),
  57(nn 1, 3). *See also* Socialism
trade, 50–52. *See also* Trade
See also Economic transition;
  Privatization
Lipton, David, 18, 35(n8)
Living standards
  and Bulgaria, 25
  and debt service, 123
  in Poland, 14(n3), 24
  and socialist legacy, 3, 19
  transition and deterioration of, 2, 27,
    46, 109
  See also Economic decline

Management, business, 39, 55
Market, future of Soviet, 71–72, 74
Market economy
  and Hungary, 9
  and joining Europe, 93
  types of, 17, 34(n1)
  See also Economic transition
Markovic Program, 26
"Marshall Aid," 108–111, 116(n8)
Mazowiecki, Tadeusz, 14(n3), 19
Middle East, 53. *See also* Gulf war
Moisi, Dominique, 100
Mongolia, 14(n1)
Monopolies, 56

National Bank of Hungary, 66, 116(n5),
  121

OECD. *See* Organization for Economic
  Cooperation and Development
Oil
  and Gulf war, 59–60
  importing, 126–127
  Soviet Union and, 7, 8, 67–68,
    68(table)

Olszewski, Jan, 24, 120
Organization for Economic Cooperation and Development (OECD)
 and Poland, 21
 policy and stability concerns, 12
 trading trends within, 4
 See also West

Paris Club agreement, 104–106, 109, 122
Perestroika, 10
PHARE. *See* Poland and Hungary: Assistance in Restructuring Economies
Poland
 and Central and East European cooperation, 84
 and CMEA trade, 60, 66, 67, 76(n7)
 economic decline in, 2, 14(n3), 19, 111, 116(n6), 120
 and European integration, 52, 95, 96, 98, 99
 and foreign investment, 54, 56, 57(nn 1, 10)
 opening to West of, 6, 9
 political destabilization potential, 20, 114–115
 socialist legacy, 3
 and Soviet Union, 7, 76(n8)
 transition program in, 20–25, 32, 34(n1), 35(nn 6, 10, 12), 44, 125
 and Western assistance policy, 103, 104–106, 109, 116(n3), 122
Poland and Hungary: Assistance in Restructuring Economies (PHARE), 103, 115(n1)
Policy
 debt management, 120–124
 and economic transition, 17–34, 35(n5), 127–130, 131(nn 7, 10). *See also* Economic transition
 foreign investment, 54–55
 and privatization, 37–46
 socialist development, 5, 7, 62

Soviet collapse and future of trade, 71–75, 126–127
 trade liberalization, 50–52. *See also* Trade
 Western, 12–14, 94, 103–115, 122–124, 125–126, 129–130
Political change
 and economic decline, 3–4, 6, 14(n3)
 and economic future, 130
 and economic integration schemes, 80, 83–84
 Soviet effect on Central and Eastern European, 10
 and state-owned enterprises, 38
 and Western policy, 113, 116(n7). *See also* Stability
 See also Sociopolitical factors
Portes, Richard, 102(n10)
Prices
 Bulgarian liberalization of, 25
 CMEA and world market, 63, 75(n4)
 freezes on, 26
 and Hungarian liberalization, 122
 oil, 8
 and Polish liberalization, 21
 Russian liberalization of, 125
 for state-owned enterprises, 54
 transition and increases in consumer, 2, 37, 119. *See also* Inflation
 See also Liberalization
Private sector
 developing a, 40, 47(n5)
 and foreign investment, 55–56
 and trade liberalization, 1, 52
 Western projects to strengthen, 103
 See also Privatization; Property rights
Privatization
 difficulties of, 41–43, 47(nn 5, 9, 10, 11)
 and foreign investment, 53, 54–56, 57(n9)
 giveaway, 43–45, 47(n12), 48(nn 13, 14)
 politics of, 34, 38, 42, 54

rapid versus gradual, 37–41, 45–46, 47(n7)
role in transition of, 17–18, 37, 46(n4), 128
and socialist governments, 35(n6)
and trade liberalization, 51–52
See also Property rights
Productivity, 23(Table 1.2)
and Czechoslovakia, 31
and East Germany, 28, 29
and Hungary, 33, 51
1980s decline in, 4, 19
and Poland, 24
Russian, 126
and transition, 2
See also Economic decline
Property rights, 35(n6), 37, 46(n1). See also Privatization
Protectionism
and EC, 97–98, 100
and foreign investment, 56
and trade liberalization, 51

Redistribution, 34. See also Privatization
Reprivatization, 18, 42. See also Privatization
Resources
and debt management, 123–124
and economic transition, 128
See also Credit
Restitution, 18, 42, 121. See also Privatization
Richter, Sándor, 85
Romania
and CMEA trade, 67
and commodity shortages, 19
economic decline in, 2, 120
and European integration, 102(n5)
and foreign investment, 54, 57(nn 1, 10)
indebtedness, 6, 15(n8), 116(n6), 117(n9)
political destabilization potential, 20, 115

transition policy in, 25, 26, 34(n1), 35(n6), 48(n13)
and Western aid policy, 109
Rome Treaty, 96
Rosati, Dariusz, 18, 22
Rupnik, Jacques, 100
Russia
aid to, 13
and integration schemes, 82–83
as trading partner, 11
transition policy in, 125
See also Soviet Union

Sachs, Jeffrey, 17, 18, 21–22, 35(n8), 112
Shock therapy, 18, 34(n3), 35(n8)
and Czechoslovakia, 32
and defaulting on debt, 123
experiences with, 25–27
and Polish program, 20–25
and Russia, 125
See also Economic transition; Gradualism
Shortage economy
and 1980s decline, 19
and Polish transition program, 22
and Soviet Union, 73, 83, 125
and transition process, 2
See also Demand
Single Market, 99
Socialism
and autarky, 49–50
legacy of, 2–9, 35(n6)
Sociopolitical factors
and East Germany, 28, 30, 36(n18)
and EC membership, 97, 100–101
and foreign investment, 53–54
and Hungarian transition, 34, 122
and intraregional cooperation, 90
and Polish transition program, 24
and preference for Western trade goods, 85
and privatization, 34, 38, 42, 54
and Soviet transition, 124–125

and transition process, 2, 20, 24–25, 34, 46
See also Political change; Stability
Southeast Asia, 94, 131(n9)
Sovereignty issues, 53–54
Soviet Union
  CMEA interdependence and decline of, 6–9, 15(n12), 49, 59–75, 61(table), 68(table), 73(table), 75(n1), 76(n9)
  and commodity shortages, 19
  coup and destabilization in former, 12–13, 74, 122, 124. *See also* Stability
  Eastern bloc countries and unsettled financial issues, 67, 76(n8)
  and economic integration, 10–11, 81–83, 91–92, 92(n2), 97, 102(n5)
  and economic systems, 34(n1)
  economic transition in, 34(n4), 118(n14), 124–126
  insolvency of, 106. *See also* Debt, Soviet
  and political change in Central and Eastern Europe, 10
  and the West, 77(nn 10, 11), 114, 118(n15)
  See also Commonwealth of Independent States; Council for Mutual Economic Assistance; Russia
Stability
  and EC membership, 101
  and foreign investment, 52, 55
  and former Soviet Union, 11, 74, 82. *See also* Soviet Union
  and resolving economic crisis, 3–4
  and trade liberalization, 50, 84
  Western policymaking and, 11–14, 113–115, 122–123, 126
  See also Sociopolitical factors
Stabilization
  and EC association agreements, 99
  and foreign investment, 49
  and Poland, 20–25

role in transition of, 18–19, 30, 35(n6)
  and Russia, 125
  and Western aid policy, 108–111, 126
  See also Economic decline
Stark, David, 131(n7)
State-owned enterprises
  privatizing, 38–39, 41–46
  selling prices, 54
  See also Privatization
Subsidies
  adjustment policies and reducing, 21, 119, 121. *See also* Austerity measures
  and EC membership conditions, 97
  European agricultural, 98
  Soviet "implicit," 7, 62
Sweden, 77(n10)
Systemic transformation. *See* Economic transition

Taiwan, 40
Tariffs, 84, 96. *See also* Protectionism
Taxation
  and Hungary, 75(n2)
  Soviet export, 70–71
  and Western aid for Central and Eastern Europe, 110
Trade
  CMEA, 59–71, 61(table), 68(table), 73(table), 75(n1), 76(nn 7, 9), 77(nn 12, 13, 14, 15), 89(table). *See also* Council for Mutual Economic Assistance
  economic crisis and decrease in, 4
  and European Community, 95, 101(n3). *See also* European Community
  intraregional integration schemes, 80–92
  liberalizing, 50–52. *See also* Economic transition, trade liberalization and reorientation
  and socialist development policy, 5, 49–50

Soviet interdependence and future, 7–9, 49, 59, 69, 71–75, 126–127
Western lifting of restrictions on, 103
See also Exports; Foreign economic relations; Imports; International economy; Protectionism; Trade balance
Trade balance
  autarky and, 50
  and foreign investment, 52
  Hungarian, 121, 131(n4)
  Polish, 22–23, 24
  Soviet, 73, 73(table)
  transition targets, 50, 51
  and Western aid, 82
  See also Trade
Transition. *See* Economic transition
Tyminski, Stanislaw, 24

Ukraine, 11
Unemployment, 25(table)
  Czechoslovakian, 31
  in East Germany, 28
  Hungarian, 33, 122
  in Poland, 24, 25
  and transition process, 2, 43, 119
United Kingdom, 77(n10)
United States
  and assistance, 110, 116(n3)
  and European agricultural subsidies, 98
  trade with, 100(n3)

U.S. Federal Reserve Bank, 5

Vietnam, 14(n1)

Wages
  and Czechoslovakia, 31
  and East Germany, 29
  and Poland, 21, 24
  transition process and, 2, 39
  Yugoslavian freeze on, 26
West
  aid policy and stability concerns, 12–14, 103–115, 122–126, 129–130. *See also* Aid
  Central and West European dependence on, 5–6, 129–130
  and debt management policy, 122–124
  and financing trade imbalances, 82, 127
  policy toward former Soviet Union, 125–126
  and Soviet market, 72
  See also European Community; Investment
World Bank, 15(n9), 118(n15)
World War II, 113

Yamburg-Tengiz complex, 8, 76(n8)
Yeltsin, Boris, 125
Yugoslavia
  civil war in, 12, 100, 101, 115
  and Soviet bloc, 7, 14(n1)
  transition program in, 26